One. Little. Pill.

My Journey from Addiction and Darkness to Purpose and Light

Deb Lawless-Miller

ISBN: 978-1-964143-01-9

Suncoast Digital Press, Inc.
Sarasota, Florida

www.suncoastdigitalpress.com

Printed in the United States of America

Dedicated to Hunter,
my reason for everything.

While this book is based on actual events,
certain individuals, entities, characterizations,
incidents, and locations were changed
to protect the privacy of individuals.

Contents

"It always seems impossible, until it is done."

—Nelson Mandela

Foreword

Linda Remley Gorman
Certified Addictions Professional
Trauma Resolution Practitioner

I've heard countless stories detailing the horrors of addiction and its consequences. One of those stories is my own. Deb Lawless-Miller's story in *One. Little. Pill.* is both typical and extraordinary at the same time. If you or someone close to you is struggling with addiction, today or in the past, Deb's story will hold you, touch you, and leave you with hope. Importantly, this book will raise awareness among all of us in today's world of skyrocketing opioid crises.

I am a grateful, recovering addict with 43 years of sobriety. I have been in recovery from alcoholism and substance abuse since mid-1981. Being told I had a chronic, progressive, and potentially fatal illness caused me to seek education in the field of addiction. I went on to pursue a career in assisting others, becoming a Certified Addictions Professional, while continuing to devour information on the topic.

In 2017, I chose to focus all my energy on preventing veteran suicide through trauma resolution using neuroscience-based techniques. I've witnessed one powerful outcome after another. Equally useful is a practice of leading veterans and their families towards a life that is so personally fulfilling that the idea of self-harm—including detrimental use of alcohol or other substances—becomes out of the question. I continue this very rewarding work today with Operation Warrior Resolution in Sarasota, Florida.

As with veterans, Deb's story reminded me how easy it is to go from never considering yourself a likely candidate for becoming an addict to finding yourself underwater. In 2019, I had minor surgery to remove a ganglion cyst from my wrist area, a problem I'd also had before due to overuse… probably from exercising with a rowing machine or planking during pure barre classes. The physician had removed fluid as a possible solution prior to suggesting surgery. I agreed to the operation, with the understanding that I'd likely be able to return to work that same afternoon.

As part of my outpatient pre-operation process, the nurse stood with a prescription pad in hand and asked me if I had a preference for a pain reliever. "Like what?" I asked, somewhat confused. "I was told this would not be very painful." She rattled off a few drug names; the only one I recognized was *oxycodone* and I recoiled as if she'd offered me a rattlesnake! I quickly replied, "How about I just take regular Tylenol and let you know how it goes?"

She smirked and said, "Oh, you must have a high pain threshold."

"No, it's pretty much the opposite. I have a low pain threshold. I don't even tolerate discomfort well—ask my husband."

When she said nothing but kept her smirk, I went on to say, "Are you not aware of the opioid epidemic in this country? Do you not know how highly addictive these drugs are? Haven't you heard that deaths from opioid overdose are at an all-time high in our area and throughout the US? I wouldn't take an opioid unless it were the absolute last resort and I was hospitalized for the pain." The smirk disappeared as she looked a little taken aback at the vehemence of my response.

I'd read the news reports; I'd seen the statistics. Why wasn't everyone treating this situation as seriously as warranted? Now, a few years later, it seems everyone I know has been affected by these sad statistics—they lost a teenage son or daughter to opioids, or they have had to console a friend or family member who has been directly affected by prescription pain pill abuse or misuse.

I believe that putting a face and a personal story on this issue is what is required to bring the public's attention to the devastation of opioid addiction. Deb's story is very moving, both in the frightening days and in the recovery years. She invites us into her personal point of view as a survivor of this epidemic. Deb clearly demonstrates the conflict between values and behavior that every active addict struggles with as they continue to deteriorate into a waking nightmare of using, scheming to find more supply, flaunting formerly deeply held convictions, and betraying themselves and everyone else in their circle of influence.

It was frankly heartbreaking to read parts of this even knowing that she did recover and today enjoys what I would call a full recovery. Deb generously describes the measures she took to reduce shame, request interdependence with people seeking a spiritual basis for living, and to develop the kind of internal strength and resiliency that makes her a role model for recovery today.

I urge you to educate yourself about the opioid epidemic, to become part of the solution, to foster a society where addiction is less likely to occur. I believe you'll be motivated by Deb's story just as she has been motivated to remain clean and sober no matter what.

"You can't go back and change the beginning,
but you can start where you are and change the ending."

—C. S. Lewis

One. Little. Pill.

Introduction

Where It All Began

One. Little. Pill.

Many addicts will tell you that they knew early on that they were addicts. One of my friends started popping pills at five years old after watching her much older sister take them. She said that, even then, she knew she liked the feeling, even though she couldn't identify it. I, on the other hand, would never have imagined that this was my fate. In my high school years, sure, I loved a good party and feeling buzzed from a few beers, but I didn't crave alcohol the next morning or even every night—it was a social thing. I was already a low-energy person and struggled with depression, so an alcohol-induced hangover was not worth the mental anguish. At that time, decades ago, I was clueless about the jungle of beasts that occupy the space between drinking and not drinking alcohol. Now I know that there are countless ways to numb out painful emotions, get high, and avoid life's sharp edges.

Turn back the clock. I am 23 years old and my head is pounding with a horrific hangover when a friend offers me a Vicodin to curb the misery. As soon as I feel the melting away of my excruciating aches and pains, replaced with the sweet rush of euphoria, there is no turning back. That one little pill changes my life forever.

College is a few years behind me and I'm marrying a man I've known since childhood. The union makes perfect sense. Trevor and I had a similar upbringing, have many of the same friends, and we fit into each other's families brilliantly. And that's not all we have in common. We both have an obsessive love of Vicodin.

It started out with us taking a few on the weekend to relax and unwind. Some people could handle that and not even think about wanting more. However, if you have the propensity for addiction, taking a few pills on the weekend quickly turns into, "Thursday is almost the weekend, so let's have one with a glass of wine." And then, "Mondays really suck, so I'll just take one to get through."

Yes, I'm now planning my entire week based on how many pills I have left and how to get more. It's the 90's, and the internet has not yet evolved for instant, updated connectivity and tracking, so Trevor and I are able to rely on a few unsuspecting doctors to write us prescriptions. Our drug use is soaring and now I am depending on the pills to get me through each day.

I manage to function (well enough) at my job at a home healthcare company that supplies equipment and services to hospice patients, many receiving end-of-life care in their homes. I am now stealing from co-workers that I know have painkillers (for legitimate use) just sitting in their purses, daring me to take a few.

Today, a pal at work and I are discussing our mutual appreciation of opioids (me, never admitting I am taking a fist-full every day), when he shows me his stash: a humongous bag filled with all types of pills! "How did you get these?" I ask, trying not to sound too ecstatic.

"When a patient dies, I go out to their house to pick up our equipment and I grab any medications they were taking. Only the good shit, of course. Here, take some," he says, tossing the bag to me.

"How do you know what's what?" I ask.

"What are you looking for?"

"I'll take any Vicodin or Percocet you've got." He takes the bag back and rifles through it. He hands me a handful of Percocet. I look at the nearly 30 pills in my hands and feel my heart beating faster as I contain my giddy delight and calmly say, "Okay, thanks."

"Keep this our secret and you are welcome to share with me," my coworker-turned-drug dealer responds, and off he goes.

Not all, but most of our patients are on hospice or have terminal diseases that cause them tremendous pain. We usually lose two or three patients every month, so my pal and I have a steady supply. I keep my newfound "friend" and our mutual understanding from my husband. And so begins my life of addiction and matching behavior—that is, a life of lies.

Even though I am high every minute of every day, my husband has no idea. It never occurs to him that I am in trouble because he assumes I am only taking pills when we are together. I have two reasons for not sharing my secret. One is because I don't want to share my supply. It's as simple as that. Secondly, I know he would go ballistic if he knew I had shared the secret about our drug habit with a stranger. But mostly, it is because I don't want to share. My inventory is my security. It feels like my life depends on it being there, and I will not give up that sense of control.

A gravy train never goes on forever. I've enjoyed my easy pill procurement for six months, but I just got some big news; my co-worker has gone into a rehab center. *Good for him, terrible for me*, I think. I have enough pills to get me through this week, but I know that I am going to soon be in trouble.

It's Friday night and I take my last handful of Percocet. I tell myself that my pill use is simply over: I quit. I fall asleep and wake up craving drugs. For the next five days, I am violently ill from the withdrawal. When the vomiting stops, I am so weak I cannot get out of bed. I fall, high-speed like a charred meteor, into a deep and dark depression. I am out of work for three weeks and now my job is on the line. I've lost so much weight and my eyes are so dark and sunken, I am hard to look at. My husband is terrified as I beg him to kill me. I cannot take the emotional pain, much less the physical pain I am experiencing. I am in hell.

Instead of killing me to put me out of my misery, he throws me in the car and drives me to a doctor's appointment he's made on my behalf. He knows that if he brought me to the ER, they would most likely put me in a psych ward and there would be no denying my mental health issue (i.e., depression) to family and friends. What he doesn't know is that I am coming off of a 6-month binge of narcotics.

The physician is kind. Without me having to share my dirty secret, he declares that I have a heck of a stomach bug, says that I seem to be on the mend, and is ready to send me off. "What about her wanting to die?!?" Trevor asks, absolutely flabbergasted at the doctor's dismissiveness.

"Oh, yes. That's right...let's start her on Prozac and see how she does," Doc says.

I am finally starting to feel normal again, having been off painkillers for a few months. The anti-depressants are working, and I am free from the clutches of the opioids. I assume Trevor is, too, and that should help me a lot. I have a new job that is closer to home, and life is grand. We are both in such a good space that we decide it is time to start our family. Within no time, I am pregnant and elated beyond description. Calls are made to our families and plans are made for a larger house. Like most first-time pregnant moms, my every thought and action is about the baby, day and night. Trevor is over the moon, so excited about becoming a dad. All our conversations are about this wonderful new chapter starting for us.

But the highest highs seem to always be followed by the lowest lows. Nearly at my first-trimester mark, I am at work when the bleeding starts, light at first. I desperately try to keep myself calm, attempting to recall if I'd heard or read that this is normal. I surely have read enough about pregnancy to know, but in my gut, I can feel the wheels starting to come off.

I leave the bathroom and approach my co-worker, Eileen, who is in the seventh month of her first pregnancy. She's the only one at my workplace who I've told I'm expecting. Anything she's shared (like when she feels her baby kick) fills me with excited anticipation for my own miracles. Now in tears, I ask her, "Did you ever have spotting in your first trimester?"

She pauses, thinking, and says, "Yes, I remember having a few days of light bleeding...it's pretty common, I think." As soon as the words come out of her mouth, I feel a pain shoot through my abdomen so severe that I think someone has stabbed me. I let out a cry and double over. I manage to get back to the bathroom to the toilet before hemorrhaging starts. There is so much blood and clots. There is no denying I am having a miscarriage.

When Eileen comes in after she's called my doctor, she quietly tells me that the doctor wants to see me as soon as I can get there. "What do I do about *this*?" I ask, looking through tears down into the bowl where my unborn baby is, somewhere in all that blood.

With tears welling, she says, "You need to flush it, honey."

───── ──◇── ─────

The dark veil engulfs me once again. I cry for weeks and dream every night about me flushing my baby down the toilet. My head understands what happened; miscarriages are common in first pregnancies. It was nothing that I did wrong, I am sure of that. But my heart is broken with a wound so deep, I cannot begin to imagine it ever mending. The only comfort for me is knowing that I am able to get pregnant with Trevor, and that, most likely, the miscarriage was a one-time occurrence.

Now, I'm emotionally ready to try again. Month after month, we wait anxiously for another positive pregnancy test. Over and over, we only receive negative results. After a stressful eight months of failure, we are seeking professional help. A close friend has recommended an infertility doctor and we set an appointment.

Dr. Lou is larger than life, with beautiful energy that radiates through him. He has a light within him that shines so brightly you can't help but feel encouraged. Dr. Lou reviews our medical questionnaire and declares that we should have no issue getting pregnant naturally, and that we simply need to give it more time. "Come back in four months if you are still not pregnant," he says cheerfully and sends us on our way.

When we walk into his office four months later, still not pregnant, I feel desperate. There are dozens of fertility tests that can diagnose many potential issues that can keep a couple from procreating. The first test is usually a semen analysis. They ask for a sample and observe the sperm under a microscope to test sperm count and motility. Dr. Lou calls us into his office and shows us the live sperm projected onto a computer screen from a microscope. There are clearly millions of them; however, they are all clumped together and barely moving. "See here?" Dr Lou asks while pointing with his pen. "These little guys aren't swimming. They are all just stuck together. Looks like you have anti-sperm antibodies."

I have no idea what that means, but I can tell from the look on Dr. Lou's face that it's not good news. His jolly demeanor is gone; now he's quiet as if preparing us for heartbreaking news. Which he is. He starts off with the good news. "Luckily, Trevor, your body does generate sperm. Millions of them. Unfortunately, there are antibodies in your semen, which means your body is viewing your sperm as invaders and is trying to kill them. Your immune response is causing the sperm to die."

Trevor asks what I, too, want to know, "So, does this mean we cannot get pregnant?"

Dr. Lou responds optimistically, "Deb will be able to get pregnant with her egg and your sperm. However, we will be using a procedure called ICSI—intracytoplasmic sperm injection—where we inject the sperm directly into her egg. Once the egg is fertilized, we transfer it back into the uterus."

Sounds simple enough, I'm thinking. *Sign us up!* What we do not realize or expect when we start this journey is the extremely high cost of the procedure, both emotionally and financially. But we are willing to do whatever we have to, at any expense.

———◇———

The more eggs my body produces in a cycle, the better my chances. Every day for two weeks, I inject myself with hormones to help increase the number of eggs, which will eventually become fertilized with Trevor's sperm. I'm told that once they determine my eggs are present, I will give myself another shot called the "pregnancy hormone" or hCG (*human chorionic gonadotropin*).

Now it's time for the doctor to perform a procedure they call "harvesting" my eggs, retrieving them from my uterus and placing them in their temporary home, a petri dish. They inject each with

Trevor's sperm and after one week, the surviving, healthy zygotes are transferred into my uterus. The plan is that at least one will attach and thrive. Now I wait, praying continuously for a positive pregnancy test.

Although the IVF procedure seems straightforward, trust me when I tell you it is a life-changing experience. The stress of all the appointments and timing to make sure my body was producing everything it should did a number on my psyche and relationship with my husband. Not to mention, all the extra hormones I injected blew up my emotions.

Sitting in the fertility clinic's waiting room for endless appointments (often several in a week), the energy in the room is heavy and heartbreaking. I realize the other women are just as desperate as I am in this life-or-death journey. It is an experience I would not wish on anyone, and I will always remember the angst, sadness, and fragile hope in that room.

Nine months later, we experience the miracle of life, blessed with a healthy baby boy.

———— ◇ ————

I discover that Trevor is still using and abusing opioids. *My* painkillers, in fact. My son was delivered through a surgical procedure called a "Caesarian" or "C-section," so recovery can be quite painful. Trevor refused to let me hold onto the bottle of Percocet I had been given by the obstetrician. Surprisingly, I am content to take them as directed and even less than prescribed. I am breastfeeding and fear our baby son Hunter could be affected, so I switch to Tylenol as soon as I can. I am walking towards the crib, bend over to pick up a diaper from the box on the floor, and WHAM! The pain strikes me like a lightning bolt. I slowly make my way to the medicine cabinet.

My pain meds are nowhere to be found. Trevor is out of town for work, so I call him. "Hey, I did something to my abdomen. I'm in so much pain, I can't stand up. Where are the Percocets?"

His reply is cold and defensive. "You don't need a Percocet, take a Tylenol," he snaps.

I start to panic. "Trevor, I literally cannot stand up! I won't be able to pick up the baby from the crib when he wakes up. Where is the bottle of my Percocet?!"

But I know where they are. I know how addiction works. I know they are gone. "I have no idea where they are," he says and hangs up. My heart sinks, but I'm not ready to give up.

I tear through Trevor's home office and find bottles of Vicodin, Percocet, and Oxycodone—all empty. Buried in this graveyard is my 30 Percocet prescription, which was filled only five days ago. Also empty.

I now have to deal with my pain as well as figure out how to take care of Hunter. Then I'll need to figure out what the hell Trevor is up to and deal with this new situation. But that's tricky.

If I confront him with the evidence, I will be admitting that I went into his office and tore through his personal space. Over the last few months, I've noticed that Trevor's fuse is shorter than normal, and his temper is quick to flare. I attributed it to the stress of anticipating parenthood, then having a newborn at home, and of course, lack of sleep—but now I know he is on edge about his dark secret. If I were dealing with a stable, non-violent husband, I would have no fear of confronting him. However, I have experienced his temper in the past, and I cannot risk igniting it again now that our newborn baby is in the house.

I decide to do what I must in order to keep the peace. I sweep this issue under the rug with my well-worn broom used for that purpose, so to speak. For the next seven months, I watch as my husband slips deeper and deeper into the addiction. He is no longer capable of being a good employee, husband, or father. His work performance has tanked. He is no longer the top producer in his sales job and he misses flights to company meetings. He doesn't show up for sales calls when he is passed out from the Xanax he takes to help him sleep after taking Adderall and opioids all day.

And now it's the last straw. He's out of town on business. His boss goes to Trevor's room since he's not shown up for their meeting and is not answering his phone. From the hotel hallway, he hears several alarms going off. Fearing that something tragic has occurred, he has the hotel manager open the door to the room, where he finds Trevor.

Passed out from the pills, he did not hear the multiple blaring alarms going off, nor the banging on the door. Finally, after being shaken violently, he wakes up. He gives a lame excuse, showers, and starts his day. His boss is quite upset and later asks Trevor if he needs help.

I truly believe that if Trevor had been honest at that moment and accepted some help, his life would have turned out differently—and better for all of us.

He denies having a problem and says no thanks to any help. A week goes by and he is fired.

Trevor's job loss is shaping the trajectory of our little family's path. And instead of making his job hunt a priority, he spends the majority of every day playing golf. He stays out late and leaves Hunter and me on our own. I have no paying job, and now he doesn't either; but instead of acting appropriate to that dire fact, Trevor is spending money like crazy.

He assures me that we have plenty of money in savings to cover our bills until he gets a new job. It's Saturday morning, and as I watch him drive off to his golf game in a new BMW, I'm thinking about his new golf clubs, expensive wine, and new clothes he bought for himself.

But I see "past due" notices on our mortgage and cars. I cannot imagine bringing it up, as I know he would fly off the handle. Even considering it makes my anxiety sky-rocket. I feel trapped, afraid, and very alone.

I look at Hunter, sitting in his high chair, happily eating his banana. I see the $100 bottle of wine on the kitchen counter. *Fuck it.* I go into Trevor's stash that he doesn't realize I know about. I place the lovely little white pill on my tongue. I open the wine and take a swig right out of the bottle. Minutes later, as the euphoria washes over me, all the anxiety and emotional distress disappears. I sense a burst of energy I haven't felt in a long, long time. I think, *Yes, I am finally safe.*

CHAPTER

1

Do I Really Have a Problem?

I do not want to be a drug addict. More than anything, I do NOT want to be a drug addict. I picture drug addicts as dirty, immoral, and pitiful. They live in squalor and make their money from stealing from unsuspecting people. They are so lowly that they turn to prostitution or dealing drugs just to support their habit. I think most of them are born into families of addicts who live in crowded cities in government housing. There is no way I am one of them! But now it's 3 a.m., I'm awake, uncomfortable, and irritated—and I know the only way back to sleep is to take a few Vicodin. In the pre-dawn dark and shadowy room, I sit on the edge of the king-size bed I share with my husband, and it dawns on me—I am physically dependent on opioids.

I am terrified. I know I cannot stop on my own, yet I am still not willing to admit defeat. My brilliant, drug-dependent mind and body keep telling me that I can manage this life as long as I take the pills in moderation. I can maintain this. I figure that "only" five Vicodin and five Adderall a day will prevent me from being sick, as well as keep me under the radar of the doctors and pharmacies that I shop. Yes, I will have to cut my usage in half in order to get to the 5/5 a day, but I figure I can handle it—after all, I'm not that far gone. I'm not like, you know, a *drug addict.*

I still live with Trevor, but the marriage has fallen into pieces. The intense raging is so bad that my neighbors hear him screaming at me almost nightly. I live in constant fear of physical abuse, as well. I keep all of this home drama as secret as possible, assuming I am succeeding until the day that my one-year-old calls the police.

Little Hunter and I are home alone when he picks up the phone and accidentally calls 911. I'm busy in the kitchen when the police and fire trucks show up, engines blaring. When they learn that the call was a toddler's mistake and everything is okay, off they go. About 20 minutes later, my neighbor knocks on my door.

Stacy's a sweet woman, about my age. She and her husband moved in next door within weeks of us, so we became fast friends. This morning, she looks disheveled and is as white as a ghost. "Hi!" I greet her with a hug and when I pull away, I see she is crying. "Oh no...what happened?" I ask as she enters the foyer.

"Is Trevor home?" she asks.

"No, I honestly have no idea where he went. What's wrong?" I ask as my stomach starts to turn. *Did she see him out with another woman? Did he do something crazy to them?*

My mind is reeling when she blurts out, "I—I saw the police and fire truck here and my first thought was, he finally did it. He killed her." She burst out sobbing, and my head starts spinning. I can't grasp what she is talking about. Then she says, "Deb, I know this is none of our business, but Dave and I can see through to your house, and we see how he screams at you and hurts you. We decided not to talk to you about it because we didn't want to embarrass you, but when we saw EMS here, we really did think he had killed you!'

Hunter is holding his favorite truck and standing at my side, looking up at us as we hug and I assure her we are okay. "Sure, he has a bad temper, but he has never and would never hurt Hunter...and I'm okay, really."

"I am so afraid for you and Hunter," Stacy says. "Please let us help you."

"It sounds much worse than it is," I promise her. She looks at me, turns and leaves.

I know I can't tell Trevor about the conversation because he would never accept it. He would accuse me of telling Stacy a bunch of lies to make him look bad. He never wants me talking to anyone, and

12

honestly, I don't want anyone to see behind the curtains, either. Best that everyone thinks we have it all together. My shame fuels my denial. My denial fuels my shame. My drugs are my smoke screen that helps keep the truth hidden and distant.

I finally tell my parents about Trevor. I admit the abuse to them about six months after hearing "…we thought he had killed you" from Stacy.

It is before dawn and Trevor jacks me against the wall by my throat while his fist is raised and positioned to come down on my face. His eyes are black with rage, and I instinctively know that if I let out the slightest noise, that will give him a reason to choke me. "I am going to fucking kill you," he whispers in my ear. And I believe him.

The difference between this time and all of the others is that I am holding Hunter in my arms when I'm attacked. With horror, I realize that he would hurt me right there with no care at all that our precious son would witness it from inches away.

And if he doesn't care about having Hunter witness this, then nothing will stop him from killing me. Hunter starts to cry. With one hand, Trevor softly strokes his cheek and says, "It's okay buddy, you're okay." The other hand stays firmly around my throat. Finally, he releases me and tells me to go to bed. About an hour later, I open the bedroom door to find him asleep on the couch.

The crime I had committed, which sent him into such rage and ultimately ended our marriage, was my failure to notice there wasn't an extra roll of toilet paper in the bathroom.

Now hurrying, I pack a bag for myself and Hunter, quietly pick up my son, put my dogs on their leashes, and slip out of the house. I don't want to risk the sound of the garage door waking Trevor up, so I leave without a car. It's now 5 a.m. and the garbage men are picking up trash when I run by them, barefoot, with a toddler and two dogs in tow.

My parents live a block away. Dad is awake when I come in through the garage. He is obviously stunned to see me and my entourage at this hour. I hand Hunter to him and frantically run around the house, closing blinds and locking doors. "What's going on, honey?" Dad asks.

By this time, the commotion has woken my mom. When they finally get me to stop locking the doors and windows, I stutter, "He is going to kill me."

There is no turning back now. The cat is out of the bag, and under no circumstances can it get back in the bag. I tell my parents everything (sans my own "minor" pill problem). Within an hour, Trevor shows up.

He is calm and kind when my dad opens the door. "Hey, George. Can I have a minute to talk to Deb?" I hear him ask, quite respectfully. Trevor and my parents have always had a close relationship. We spend a lot of time together, and they love him like a son. Since they had never witnessed his rage towards me, or anyone for that matter, it is hard for them to understand what's happening. However, there was no denying that whatever happened that morning was real and had terrified me.

"That's not a good idea, Trevor," I can hear Dad say, though I am around the corner in another room. "She is really upset. I don't know what happened, but I have never seen someone as scared as she was this morning. I think you should give each other some space."

"Fine," Trevor says, "but tell her we need to talk and I want Hunter home by five this afternoon, or I am coming back to get him myself."

Suddenly I am in such a predicament. First, I am not going to let Hunter go with him. If he comes back, it will be an awful scene and traumatic for Hunter. Secondly, I need to get more pills without him knowing. This means I either need Trevor asleep or out of the house so I can find his hiding spot and grab some Vicodin. I need to get back into our house.

The power of addiction is enormous. The disease causes us to shift our priorities to make us believe that nothing is more important than feeding our habit. I would never go back into that house like that if I wasn't addicted to opioids. I should have the police with me while I go in and pack up things for Hunter and myself.

I should wait until I get a restraining order. It makes no sense for me to insist to my parents that I have to go to my house, today, alone. But my addiction is calling the shots now.

By mid-afternoon, I am thinking of nothing else but how I am going to get more pills. I start to feel irritable and discontent. The constant questioning about my "plan" is making me crazy and I can feel the nausea creeping in. When you start feeling the withdrawal symptoms, your perspective on everything changes. I finally talk my parents into letting me leave Hunter with them while I go back alone "to talk to Trevor."

To my surprise and glee, Trevor's not home. Quietly, I check all the rooms to make sure he is in fact gone, and then I race around to all the hiding spots. Nothing. My heart is pounding as I frantically look everywhere I can think of to find his stash. I open drawers, paw through closets, look under beds and mattresses. My head is pounding, and I can feel the pain taking over my muscles as the withdrawals set in. The physical craving is overtaking my fear of getting caught (or worse) by Trevor coming in. I search high and low with reckless abandon.

I hear the front door. *Shit.* I had promised I would call my parents when I arrived to say I was okay, but I've been so engulfed in looking for the pills that I forgot. Worried, my father shows up unannounced. When I answer the door, I am pale and shaking. "Where is he?" Dad asks, assuming Trevor is the cause of my distress.

"He isn't here. I don't know where he is."

"Why didn't you call to let us know you are okay? You scared us to death!" he scolds.

"I'm sorry, I got here and started packing and now I don't feel well, so I wanted to hurry up before he got home," I say, feeling the hot flashes take over. And now we both hear the garage door open. "Dad, give me a minute with him," I say, pleading. "I promise to call you in ten minutes. If I don't, you can come back."

Dad leaves through the front door, and Trevor enters through the garage side door. He takes one look at me and assumes my frazzled state is because of his behavior. He comes close to hug me and tell me how sorry he is. I hug him back. Again, we're back on the roller coaster. He pulls away from me, and that's when I notice the bag he's holding. CVS. He just came from the pharmacy! *Thank you, God!* I think, and pray there is a prescription in that bag.

Trevor tosses the bag into his office and says, "I will be right back." He heads into the bathroom, and I dash for the bag. I am elated to find a bottle of Norco 10/325, quantity 90. I empty a handful into my pocket and pop two into my mouth. I am so relieved to have them. I'm not even thinking about my escape this morning or the mess we're in. I'm just happy to start feeling okay again. I calmly greet Trevor as he returns and we decide we'll go get Hunter. He drives us over to my parents and waits in the car while I go inside.

I put on my "everything is fine now, really" face. My parents do their best to talk me into staying with them for a few more days. "Just give yourself some time to digest what has just happened." I know they are worried sick about us going back to a volatile atmosphere, but I manage to calm their fears with promises of frequent check-ins.

I pick up Hunter and head back to the car. To him. To the danger zone. To crazy town. To my drug supply.

It's not long before Trevor notices the missing pills from his supply and all hell breaks loose. Of course, I deny his accusation of stealing, but he does not believe me. I am quickly reminded of the chaos, fear, and danger I have chosen to walk back into.

It is the next day that I start ordering my own supply of opioids off the internet, which is risky in a multitude of ways. First, I never really know if I am getting legitimate opioids or something laced and sinister.

But I don't care about any of the risks, including that the pills are outrageously expensive, and I know it is only a matter of time until Trevor notices the high credit card bill. I know I have to come up with another way to feed my addiction. And then, the most wonderful thing happens—I develop a severe case of shingles.

Shingles is caused by a virus (the same one as from having chickenpox) which attacks nerves in my body and is extremely painful. Not only is the pain unbearable, but my skin also breaks out in an unsightly rash. For me, it occurs on the trigeminal nerve, which is located on my face, just outside of my ear. I have an unsightly, angry, bubbling rash that sends me into excruciating pain if there is the slightest sensation. As terrible as this diagnosis is, I feel like I hit the jackpot. Every doctor I see is more than happy to write me a prescription for painkillers. I line up appointments with different doctors for weeks on end, showing them my blisters and crying out in pain. Every doctor knows about shingles and the pain it causes, and to see the rash gives them no doubt that my need for painkillers is legit. I score over 20 prescriptions from doctors all over the state.

———◇———

My first encounter with the law is not as bad as it should be, and is definitely not the wake-up call I need. I am asked by a detective to "come down to the station" for a few questions. They are very vague, and, in my drug-addled mind, I figure the conversation they request will be something regarding my soon-to-be ex-husband, who has also become addicted to opioids and is facing some legal issues. I arrive at the station at 7 p.m. with my three-year-old son asleep in his car seat. I scoop him up and walk into the station, holding him with his head resting on my shoulder. "I am here to see Detective Marlin," I tell the officer at the front counter.

In half a minute, two detectives are escorting me to a back room where they present me with a very poorly forged prescription for Norco 10/325. "We received a call from CVS on Main Street, letting us know you are passing bad prescriptions. Is this yours?" Detective Marlin asks.

"Yes," I reply, "but I didn't forge that. My doctor gave it to me." In fact, it is a legit prescription—except the quantity has been changed. I feel very clever changing the quantity of 30 to 80 and probably would have gotten away with it had it not been an odd quantity. Usually, Rx's are written for monthly supplies of 30, 60, or 90; the quantity of "80" set off all kinds of alarms.

I am not sure why the detectives let me go without any repercussions; they clearly know I am lying and have committed a felony. But they give me a stiff warning "not to do that again" and off I go. I suspect it is because they see Hunter sleeping in my arms and decide it would be best for the innocent child not to bear witness to his mother being arrested and then be torn from her arms. Whatever the reason, I am relieved and grateful to be free and learn another valuable lesson (aside from paying attention to the quantity): if I take my child with me to get forged prescriptions filled, they are less likely to arrest me.

This is my first lesson on how a pharmacist can become suspicious that a highly addictive medication's prescription may have been forged. I try again. This time I gave a smaller amount and slightly different directions.

Do you recognize the warped thinking of an addict? A close call with being thrown in jail and convicted as a felon does NOTHING to slow me down. The lessons I deem valuable are only what could be useful to avoid arrest and continue to feed my habit.

After that first encounter with the law, I am arrested several more times; luckily, my son is never with me. During one of my arrests, I ask the detective if they would have arrested me if I had my young son in tow. "Absolutely," he replies. "I just brought in a mother with her four young children in the car. She was also trying to pass a fake prescription, which in this state is a felony. Plus, she was driving under the influence with her kids, so she had to be held accountable." I picture the scene and how traumatized the kids must have been, seeing their mom taken away by the police. After that, Hunter never comes with me.

By the time I go to inpatient rehab, I have six felonies. Yes, indeed, I have a problem.

The second time I am arrested, I am divorced and living with my son at my parent's house. I am not home when the police arrive and inform my parents that there is a warrant out for my arrest and that I have two choices: I can turn myself in, or, they will continue to look for me and they will arrest me wherever and whenever they find me.

It feels like a knife in your heart when your own mother stops believing you, stops protecting you. Before the police come, she has learned that I am going to be arrested because of the prescription I filed under my friend's husband's name; however, she does not share her knowledge with me or my dad. You can imagine what I walk into when I arrive after the police have come to their home.

"Deb," she says, "you have a problem here and you need to either admit it and get help or face the consequences." I am told about the police visit and my "two options." My dad's facial expression is one of deep, pained sadness. He says nothing. Mom is the one who is standing up to the addict part of me, firm in her conviction that I must now face the music. I am irritated at how confrontational and unsympathetic she is. Yes, I know I have a problem, and I am going to extremes to feed my habit, but I am scared to death. I feel vulnerable and completely exposed. It is impossible for me to look directly at my dad or mom. I am drowning in fear and shame.

I finally admit defeat and agree to turning myself in. The excuse I use for my bad behavior is that I am still in pain from the case of shingles, and my doctor has stopped prescribing pain meds for me. "No one believes me!! I am in so much pain!" I wail, while holding my hand to the cheek where the blisters had once been, the skin now perfectly clear. "I would never have to resort to this if my doctor would just give me a higher dose of pain meds!"

Regardless of my excuse, off I go to turn myself in. Where I passed the illegal prescription is a small, sleepy town that does not have the capability of processing a criminal like me, so they send me to the State Police Department. The atmosphere and décor say *government*—grey cinderblock, hard metal chairs, and a clock that looks like the one in my second-grade classroom, ticking off each second. Click. Click. Click.

I am read my rights, fingerprinted, given a court date, and sent on my way. This isn't so bad, I tell myself. (By my sixth arrest, I am not so unfazed, and I am starting to experience the consequences of my bad choices. The cinderblock walls close in.)

When you live in a small town, everyone reads the local newspaper—especially the Obituaries and the Police Logs. It is in that crime report section of the local Sunday paper where just about everyone who knows me and my family finds out that I have been arrested.

I am suddenly a big foul fish in a small pond, the one everyone stares at and talks about.

My poor parent's phone rings off the hook. Most, I'm afraid, are gossipmongers, though some offer sympathy to my mom and dad. Not one single person, friend or otherwise, reaches out to me. This is punishment of the worst kind. Shunned rather than seen as a young mother in dire need, I become overwhelmed with shame.

I am not seen as a friend in need who has found herself in a dark place; I am an embarrassment to my closest friends and no longer worthy of their friendship. I develop extreme anxiety every time I have to leave the house. I can't bring my son to his friends' houses to play because I am no longer welcome. I am viewed as a drug addict, an untouchable. Certainly, no longer a person to be trusted around children. No longer a human being worthy of being acknowledged. Breaking news: Deb is a pathetic, desperate drug addict. Period.

About a month after word of my arrest gets out, I am driving home and see three of my closest friends talking to my mom in the driveway. As soon as they see my car coming, they bolt and never look back. I know at that moment that there will be no reconciliation. They have no interest in knowing what is happening to me or *why* I am resorting to illegal measures to feed my drug habit. Surely, they are full of questions, "What happened to you?" and, "Why are you doing this?" They don't ask—can't get too close to crazy, it might be contagious.

During my years in recovery, I learn other people's behavior and actions have nothing to do with the person on the receiving end, and everything to do with what is going on in their own lives. Most of the time, negative reactions come from a place of fear. But on that day, I felt like I had stepped on a land mine, my former reality blown to bits. We have been friends since we were 12 years old! We have seen each other through everything, from first loves to weddings and babies. Our kids play together like cousins, and we are like sisters. And then, just like that, I am an outsider. It is a sudden and shocking divorce.

I start spending time at my brother's house, just to get away from living under disapproving, icy gazes from neighbors, old friends, and strangers. Their disgust with me is painful, so of course I have my answer for that: I am still using and spend the majority of my time figuring out new ways to obtain prescriptions. I have no money, no job, and an expensive drug habit. The walls are closing in and I am becoming (even more) desperate. It seems my only option is to take another step into life as a criminal and steal what I cannot buy.

I begin attending realtors' open houses to rummage through medicine cabinets and grab anything close to painkillers. I befriend elderly neighbors with the pretense of helping them with small tasks and then steal their medications. I even start my own little business, offering my help to those who need errands run and light housework. I pat myself on the back for that brilliant idea. I would get paid AND have access to the medicine cabinets of unsuspecting elderly people.

The first few months of this charade, I behave myself and build trust. My clients refer me to their friends, and the next thing I know, I have a nice little business going. The more trust I develop, the more responsibilities I am given, including driving clients to doctor appointments and picking up prescriptions. It isn't long until I am helping myself to "my share" of the pills. I also have a new strategy of calling the pharmacy pretending that I am calling from my client's doctor's office to order a narcotic for them. It is a dangerous game, but my drug-fogged brain cannot comprehend this fact. All I can think about is getting more pills. The compulsion is all-consuming. Every day, 24 hours a day…how do I get more.

One. Little. Pill.

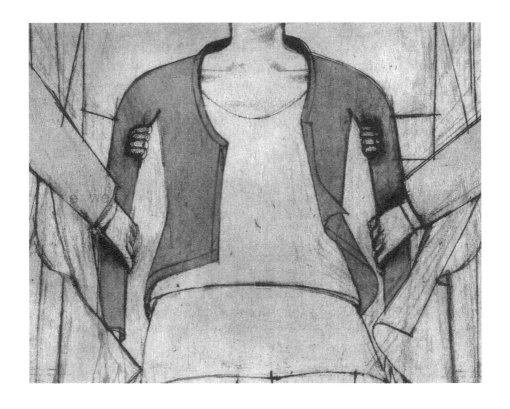

2

The Jig is Up

"Mommy? It's time to wake up." I hear Hunter's sweet little voice, and I smile. I open my eyes to see him standing next to my bed, holding a bottle of Adderall. "Here, it's time to wake up," he states again as he hands me the bottle. My heart breaks in half, realizing that he has picked up on the fact that I need to take a pill to get out of bed. This little child is watching every move I make and knows my dependence on substances in the most innocent way.

Later that day, I have my first realization about my future, and it is somber. I figure I am facing three possible outcomes: First, I could go away somewhere to kick this addiction (rehab), but the shame and embarrassment of admitting I am addicted is more than I am willing to concede, so that won't work. The second option is to overdose and take my own life. That has the appeal of avoiding truth and consequences. And the third is jail. I would rather die than go to jail, so my conclusion is I am either going to rehab, or I am going to die. My ego won't dare admit to defeat, so I had better write some letters to explain myself before my demise. I decide there will be three letters: One to my parents, another to Trevor, and a letter to Hunter.

I start with Hunter. I turn it into a little story with illustrations so he may be able to understand it more easily. The story tells of a little boy and his mom who live together and love each other very much, only the mom is sick and needs medicine to help. The only problem is, the medicine she needs to make her feel better makes her sicker. She doesn't know what to do or how to make herself feel better. The mom in the story turns into an angel who lives on the little boy's shoulder and visits his dreams at night so he can talk to her, and he is never alone. The tale tells of all the magical things they (we) would do together in his dreams and assures him he is very loved.

I picture my mom reading it to him every night and I hope it will bring him comfort. It never crosses my mind the damage I would have caused by taking my life. The disease has me believing he would be better off without me.

The letters to Trevor and my parents are filled with amends, pleading for forgiveness, and begging them to never let Hunter forget how much I love him. This option is the only thing that makes sense to me. I can't imagine living a sober life. The thought of feeling every raw emotion and drawing up the energy to get through each day without the kick of a substance is more than I am willing to experience. My diseased mind keeps telling me I am a useless human being, and that I would be even more worthless without drugs in my system.

I fold and put the letters inside a spiral notebook and hide it under the seat of my car. I'm not quite ready to follow through.

Trevor and I have been divorced for over a year and we are attempting to find common ground in our relationship. He confronts me on my arrests and addiction, urging me to get help, but I hold fast to my conviction that I don't have a problem. The lie I tell myself and to everyone:

the arrests are a misunderstanding that will be cleared up shortly.

He doesn't push the matter, he knows better. He too is running the same game, but more obvious about it. He isn't facing criminal charges, yet his inner circle has witnessed his erratic behavior. When they dare to approach the subject of his moods and substance use, they experience an onslaught of rage so full of wrath, lifelong friendships are shattered.

We tried to put the pieces back together many times before the divorce. One of our counselors suggested that Trevor's unpredictable behavior may be more than just drug use, and suggested he see a psychologist to explore the possibility of being bipolar. In the early 2000's bipolar disorder was not openly spoken about, accepted, or understood as it is today, so when the doctor confirmed this diagnosis, we were both apprehensive about his plan of care. He was immediately started on Lithium, which seemed to balance his moods and temperament. This meant he wasn't consumed with self-medicating. This worked in my favor for many reasons, mostly because I could sypher his pill supply that was no longer any interest to him. I was also relieved that our home was no longer like living on a land mine, always waiting for an explosion.

However, within weeks, Trevor stopped taking his medication, not liking the side effects of sleepiness and feeling like he was in a daze all day. Once off the Lithium, his moods spiked from deep depression to extreme hyperactivity. In attempts to balance the highs and lows, he would smoke weed. Of course. And in no time, he was back to drinking, taking Vicodin, and feeding his ego with women. Lots of women. The writing was on the wall. We were divorced within a few months.

Now we are only in relationship as Hunter's parents. We are in touch only because of him, keeping all communication surface level. I have no reason to get personal; especially since I can't risk him finding out I am abusing pills like crazy. I live in terror that he would use that to take custody from me, so I keep every contact brief. In addition, he's living with a woman who doesn't trust him, insisting he have minimal contact with me. Fine by me.

When he calls to speak to Hunter, I can easily tell if he's high and happy, or raging from lack of substances. I know to not make small talk when he calls during a down mood, but I cannot put off asking him about his lack of child support payments. This subject always enrages him, but I am overdrawn in my account—I need that money from him that Hunter and I are legally entitled to.

Oddly enough, he seems perfectly fine with my request. He asks if I'll meet him halfway between his place and mine, at a car dealer's parking lot off the main highway. "Let's meet there in an hour," he says.

I am beyond excited, knowing I will be able to deposit a check into my overdrawn account and also have enough for groceries. I strap Hunter into his car seat, and we make our way to the meeting spot. We arrive first, pull up to the fence where we'll see him arrive, and sit patiently in the car.

As soon as I see Trevor, I know immediately this is a mistake. It is Sunday afternoon, the car dealership is closed, and there is no one around. He parks behind my car, so I am trapped. I press the door lock. The car windows are down, as we were enjoying the beautiful weather. He walks to my window and tells me to get out of the car. He is clearly upset, and I know better than to oblige. Hunter is silent, sensing his dad's anger and my nervousness.

Trevor's face is red and contorted with rage. "GET OUT!!!!" He spits out the words through clenched teeth. I look in my rearview mirror, trying to see Hunter. Trevor looks in the back seat and sees our sweet little boy looking wide-eyed at him and this seems to calm him. "Hi buddy! Mommy and I need to have a conversation, so she'll be right back."

Hunter starts to cry, "No, no, Dad-deee!"

Trevor sees me attempting to close the car windows, grabs me by the hair, and starts pulling me out of the car—through the window! I hold my hair and scream for him to stop. Hunter is crying, kicking, and screaming, helpless to help his mom as he is tightly strapped into his car seat.

He manages to get me halfway out of the car window before someone pulls into the lot, notices the commotion, and drives towards us. Trevor notices them and lets me go. I drop back into my seat and quickly get the windows up. Trevor is telling the people in the car to "fuck off" and in a flash, he is gone.

I am stunned.

Hunter is bawling, and some man is knocking at my window. Mortified, I wave him off and drive home. I never ask Trevor for child support again. I now go through the state of Connecticut and leave it up to them to chase him down.

After that episode, we speak even less. I have learned what I can and cannot say, what I can and cannot ask for. I also have learned that the way he treats me is dependent on if his girlfriend at the time accepts me in his life or doesn't. I couldn't care less about them. The only thing I care about is if they are responsible enough to watch over Hunter when he is visiting his dad. Mostly, they are, but there is always a revolving door of women, so I never know what to expect on any given day.

This week, Trevor's girlfriend is a nice woman with a few kids of her own. She welcomes me and Hunter into their life, so I feel reasonably comfortable leaving Hunter with her, her kids, and Trevor at her nice home for the day. The plan is for me to then pick him up at 6 p.m. at Trevor's place, which means I have all day to work on filling a prescription. I have a few blank prescriptions from a pad I recently stole. I fill out the small form and forge the doctor's name. It's so easy.

I decide to go to a pharmacy in the town where Trevor is living, since I have not been to this particular one before. I only have a few oxys left in my current supply, so it is imperative that I fill this one. I write in the quantity for 90, an amount that will buy me 3 days of reprieve. I confidently hand the prescription over, wait and watch every move of the pharmacist. If she reaches for the phone at any time, I know she is calling the police and I will leave. She never picks up the phone, so I am surprised to see a cop walking towards me.

He quietly approaches, stops about two feet from me, and asks, "Ma'am, what is your name?"

With my throat now clenched so tight I can hardly speak, I say my name. Handcuffs are placed on my wrists and my rights are read. Everyone in the store stops to look at me. I am mortified. Until now, I have turned myself in, so I never experienced the humiliation of being arrested in public. I am brought to the police department and processed. Thankfully there is no bond set, so I am free to go after the paperwork is completed and I am given a court date.

The cop is kind and sympathetic to my situation, even though I stick to my story that the prescription is valid. Before I leave, he says, "There is no shame in admitting you have a problem and getting help. We have several men and women on our force who have had issues with addiction and alcoholism and have received help. I hope you do, as well."

I feel my face flush with embarrassment. I know he isn't buying my bullshit. Yet I have no urge to admit to anything, only to hurry up.

It is so obvious to everyone around me that I am constantly lying, but I manage to fool myself into believing I am fooling everyone else. The disease of addiction is so cunning that I am never able to see myself through the lens of those around me. Despite the crazy, irrational choices I am making, I can still convince myself that I have control over everything.

He drives me back to my car, removes the cuffs, and drives away. It is at that moment I realize he has confiscated my last two pills. Instead of being grateful I'm free as a bird, I'm angry he's "stolen" my drugs.

I immediately go into a panic. I know I am about to spiral into withdrawal. I drive to Trevor's. Thankfully, Hunter is still at the girlfriend's house finishing dinner, and not here. Trevor sees immediately that something is wrong. I know if I tell him, he'll fight for custody of Hunter, and I can't risk that.

I tell him I need to lie down; I'm not feeling well. In less than an hour I am sweating and shaking uncontrollably. He asks me over and over what I have taken, and I continue to lie. A few hours pass and I am getting worse. Assuming I am detoxing and not knowing what I have taken, Trevor grows more anxious and walks outside to search my car. He finds several empty bottles of narcotics and fears the worst. Most of the bottle labels show they are for large quantities and had all been filled in the past two weeks. And then he finds the letters.

He reads the suicide notes and calls 911, assuming I have overdosed on purpose. The next call is to my father, who hurries to me and calls my mom, who is about to board a plane, a fun trip to visit her sister for a much-needed reprieve. Once again, my addiction has hijacked the people I love the most, demanding they drop everything and pay full attention to me.

I am rushed to the hospital, where they quickly insert a tube in my throat and dispense charcoal to absorb the high levels of acetaminophen that are in hydrocodone.

Acetaminophen can severely damage the liver when taken in high doses for a long period of time. In my case, at this point, I take upwards of 15-20 pills a day which equals between 4,875-6,500 mg of acetaminophen per day. For my height and weight, the max per day for me is not to exceed 2,200 mg. I am told that 25% of my liver is severely damaged and I will be admitted to the hospital until my liver can be regenerated and a bed at a rehab is available.

I am also told that the only reason my heart does not stop with those high levels of narcotics is because the stimulant I am also abusing (Adderall) keeps it pumping.

I stay in the hospital for five days to treat my liver. Twice a day, I have to drink a solution that smells and tastes of sulfur. It is so vile that I start to gag as soon as the nurse enters the room with it. If I vomit it up (which I do many times), I have to take another shot glass full until I keep it down. Between the liver medication, the vomiting and diarrhea from detoxing, the chills, the excruciating headaches, depression, and anxiety, you would think I would be done with it all. You would think that I had learned my lesson. You would think I would not want to go through this misery again. You would think…

By the time I leave the hospital, I am physically feeling a little better (the vomiting and diarrhea have stopped), but I still feel shaky on the inside. My name is on a list for a space at a local rehabilitation center, but until a bed becomes available, I am to go into an outpatient program.

My parents are relieved, happy that I am finally getting some professional help. My lawyer is glad to be able to continue my cases and let the judge know I am in treatment. I leave the hospital on a Friday and am to start the program on Monday. Outpatient Care consists of six hours a day of addiction education, which includes group therapy and AA/NA meetings. On Saturday, I accompany my mom to the grocery store where I had previously filled prescriptions for Percocet. I tell my mom I am going to the bathroom and make a beeline to the pharmacy. "Hi," I say to the familiar pharmacist. "Do I happen to have any refills available on my Percocet prescription?"

"Let me check," she replies, and within a minute, she is back. "You have one more refill. Should I go ahead and fill it?" she asks.

"Yes, please!" I respond. "We are about done with our shopping; can you rush this?" I ask her. My heart is beating out of my chest with excitement, I am practically drooling with anticipation. In less than five minutes, I have a beautiful full bottle of Percocet and my anxiety melts away. I find my mom in the frozen food aisle, clueless as to what has just transpired. I feel extremely lucky, as only an addict could as they proceed to be the arsonist of their own life.

———◇———

Going to an outpatient program at a drug and alcohol rehab is my first introduction to Alcoholics Anonymous (AA) and Narcotics Anonymous (NA). At this point, I have surrendered to identifying as an addict: "Hi, I'm Deb, and I'm an addict." I decide to embrace my new identity and get to know my fellow addicts.

I walk into the classroom with a large coffee for me and a bag of bagels to share. It's 8 a.m. and I figure I might as well start off on the right foot by breaking bread with my fellow junkies. I was not expecting the scene that unfolds in front of me now, on my first day.

Apparently, one of the group members has just been kicked out because she tested positive on a urine test. When you enter a court-ordered program, you are subject to random urine tests to make sure you aren't drinking or drugging. This woman had lost her roll of the dice that day: She was tested, and she failed. Her probation officer was called, and off to jail she went. The members in this group have gotten to know each other and, as I would come to find out, are deeply hurt when one of their own relapses.

I am attending this program for one reason only—to convince my parents that I am not using anymore. I was high when I walked in. I manage to dodge the random urine tests because I am here by my own choosing, not by a court order. I know absolutely nothing about the disease of addiction and/or alcoholism, or how one stays clean and sober. I've never attended an AA meeting and had no clue there was such a thing as Narcotics Anonymous (NA). Our counselor asks how many days we were clean and sober, did we attend a meeting the previous night, and have we asked someone to sponsor us. "I have 23 days, I did go to a meeting last night, and yes, I have a sponsor," I lie.

A week goes by and the questions are asked again. This time, however, I lose track of how many days sober I had pretended to have, and spit out, "I have 25 days, I did attend a meeting last night, and I have a sponsor."

The counselor looks at his notes and back at me. "Seven days ago, you had twenty-three days and now you have twenty-five?" The red flag has gone up and I know my cover is about to be blown.

Raising my fingers and pretending to count on them, I say, "Oh, I mean I have thirty days!" I smile proudly. It's too late. Everyone in the room knows I am lying, and I've lost any credibility I had gained. What I don't yet realize is that people who are fighting for their lives to stay off drugs take their sobriety and clean time seriously. Every single day that they don't use or drink is a milestone to be celebrated. Not knowing my sober time is a dead giveaway that I am not clean. I decide to never come back to the outpatient program meetings.

Believe it or not, amid this controlled chaos, I manage to land a killer job in sales. In healthcare, nonetheless. I am responsible for setting up patients with home medical supplies when they leave the hospital. The beauty of this job is that I am expected to be on the road all day and not in the office, which means that I have the freedom to, once again, doctor and pharmacy shop to supply my habit. In no time at all, I am stealing prescription pads, forging the prescriptions, and guess what...getting arrested.

This time, the prescription was filled and then the cops are called. I am blissfully unaware that I have been caught and go about my day. I pick up Hunter from daycare and am just about to turn onto our street when I see two cop cars in front of the house. I drive off, my heart pounding out of my chest.

We drive around aimlessly for another hour and when I am certain they are gone, we go home. I am completely panicked, and my mind is racing. I call a neighbor who has a child Hunter's age and ask if he can play at their house for a couple of hours—because, you know, I need to go see my friend in the hospital and they don't allow young children in the I.C.U. *Lie, lie, lie.* I've gone from being a conscientious, honest person to an increasingly skillful liar, but I don't even realize this. It just doesn't register that the person I've become in order to feed my drug habit is a warped version of myself, some grotesque distortion you'd see in a house of mirrors.

Once Hunter is safe and out of sight, I call the police to see what they wanted. I pray that they will tell me that their impromptu visit had nothing to do with me. Maybe they were checking the area, looking for someone else. Yeah, right. I am informed that there is a warrant out for my arrest for forgery and that I have two options: One—I can turn myself in and pay a $1,000 bond, or two—I can show up to court on the designated date and hope and pray that the cops won't find me first.

I go for option two simply because I don't have $1,000. I don't want to sit in jail until the court date, so I just lay low for three weeks. At this point, my parents still believe I am clean and I have no intention of telling them otherwise; however, this means that I no longer have a lawyer since the last one was generously supplied to me by them. Being clean now, as far as they knew, means I have no need of a lawyer.

I figure I have been to court enough to know how the game is played: The attorney talks to the prosecutor, tells him or her that I am currently seeking treatment, and *voila!*—my case would be continued (meaning, the next hearing or proceeding would be postponed). I anticipate that all I need to do is get the attention of the prosecutor and explain my situation. No need for a lawyer, I think, *I'll be out of there in no time.* I walk into the courthouse dressed in my professional work attire; a sleeveless black dress and high heels. I leave my blazer in the car, sure that this will be a quick in and out—no need to risk wrinkles.

As I walk through the metal detectors into the courthouse, I am greeted by two detectives who are assigned to my case. The next thing I know, my wrists are cuffed. I am processed again, now for the third time, and brought to the holding cell where I will wait my turn to see the judge. Sitting there with no "officials" anywhere in sight, it begins to become clear to me why I need an attorney. Within 15 minutes of my arrival to the jail, a bus arrives and unloads 20 women from the women's State Prison. It is about 9:00 a.m. and I have no idea how long I will be here before seeing the judge. Only two things are on my mind. First, I have no pills on me as they are in the pocket of my jacket, which sits nice and unwrinkled in my car. I'll need them before too long. Secondly, I fear that my boss may be trying to reach me. How will I explain my absence? I calm myself by thinking I will be the first to see the judge and will be out in an hour, tops.

When hour three passes and I am starting to feel the sickness of the withdrawal, I know I am in trouble and start to cry. I am surrounded by women prisoners who are in orange jumpsuits as I sit quietly in my perfectly fitted Calvin Klein dress and designer heels. I feel like an absolute phony. I am all dressed up and looking like some uptown professional when inside I am no better than these women who surround me. The only difference between them and me is I had a private attorney to represent me in the past. But not today. I am a criminal and a junkie, just like them.

I hold my head in my hands and cry. I am not crying because I am scared or because I have come to some profound revelation about being an addict. No, I am crying because I feel the pain and discomfort of detox starting. I am crying for my pills.

One of the women in the next cell over keeps saying "Don't cry Momma, you're good." I have no idea what that means or what to say back.

Suddenly, there is a ruckus in the cell across from me. I look over to find a young woman staring right at me. What is horrifying is that she is completely naked and masturbating! The others in her cell are shouting at her to stop but she just keeps her eyes locked on me as she pleasures herself. I turn my back to her which makes her stop long enough to start screaming at me to turn around. I look to my cellmates for some help, but they just shrug like this is a normal occurrence. I can't believe this is happening to me.

Finally, the guard comes in to stop the madness and haul off three more inmates to see the judge. One of them is Miss Masturbates-A-Lot, which gives me some relief. I ask when I will be going upstairs to the courtroom and am ignored, of course.

It is close to one o'clock and I am in full panic mode. I am sweating and shaking and know it will only be a matter of time until the vomiting and diarrhea start. I look around my cell—dismal, cold, a metal toilet in everyone's view. *Isn't this considered inhumane?*

I am told that the judge goes to lunch between 1 and 2 p.m., so if I don't see him now, I will have to wait until after two. That would be a disaster. In addition to being absent from work and sick as a rabid dog, I will also not be able to pick up Hunter from daycare at the designated time of 4 p.m. This fact breaks me into pieces. Daycare is not his favorite place to be, and often he plays quietly by himself, just waiting for me to pick him up. The look of relief on his face when I show up would break any mother's heart. Picturing my son being so anxious, worried, and sad if I don't show up sends me over the edge. I completely lose it and demand I see the judge before lunch. Luckily, I am the last one to stand in front of him before his break.

I find out that shackles are cold and heavy and impossible to wear with high heels, yet that's how I am marched to the elevator, escorted upstairs and into the courtroom. I am shaking, sweating, and crying. The judge takes one look at me, orders the shackles be removed, scolds the guards and says to me, "Miss, you clearly don't belong in here and I don't want to see you in jail. You belong in a drug and alcohol rehab where you can get a handle on your addiction. You have three months to go into a treatment facility and get your life on track. If you come back here within those three months, you will go to jail, where, I promise, you will not be very happy." The gavel drops onto the desk and off he goes to lunch.

It takes another two hours for me to get all of the paperwork signed and processed. By the time I am done it is just after 3 p.m. I have missed all my scheduled work appointments and there are six missed calls from my boss. *Shit.* First things first. I dig my pills from their hiding spot and quickly swallow three, waiting anxiously for their effects to kick in. I know I can't drive until my shaking and nausea subside.

About 20 minutes later, my first call is to Hunter's daycare to let them know I am on my way and the next is to my boss, Tom. He picks up on the first ring. "Deb!" he says cheerfully, "what's going on?" I know this isn't a typical check-in, but more like a "Where the hell have you been all day and why didn't you answer your damn phone" conversation.

"Oh my God...you wouldn't believe what I did!" I respond back with a giggle. "I was doing some cold calling today at Hartford Hospital's Medical Building and realized about an hour ago that I left my phone at one of the doctors' offices! I literally just found it. I'm so sorry I was offline for all those hours." I hold my breath waiting for him to respond and praying he had bought my ridiculous lie.

"Well," Tom responds, "that explains why you weren't returning my calls. So, how did the cold calls go? Any luck?" Phew...bullet dodged. Or so I think.

———◇———

Three months later, I finally hit bottom after getting fired from my job. One of the detectives who had been working my case called Tom (my boss) and told him what I had been up to. Tom suspected something was off when I went missing for the entire day a few months back and had made up that stupid story. After that experience, he started tracking my cell phone to keep tabs on me. On the day the detective calls him, he reaches out and tells me I need to come into the office right away to sign some paperwork regarding my commission check. I think nothing of it and happily report to his office.

He is on the phone and waves me in. As soon as I sit down, he hands me the phone to talk to the person on the other end of the line. I assume it is someone from corporate needing information. It is not. The mystery person is Detective Adams and she informs me that the jig is up and it is in my best interest to turn myself in. I know my boss is watching my every reaction to the call, so I play it cool and simply say, "Okay," and hang up.

Tom is the first to speak. "You know you can get help for your addiction through the company, but I can't guarantee we can help with the stealing of the prescription pads." I am so humiliated and ashamed that I can't even speak. I simply stand up and walk out.

I get into my car and drive to a local library where I find a phone book (this is before internet searches) and look up local criminal defense attorneys. I call the one who has a full-color ad on the back page of the phonebook. I briefly explain what is going on, and within an hour, I am sitting in front of my new attorney, Marcus Greene.

It takes some time for Mark to get the truth out of me about how bad my addiction is. I tell him about my time in the jail in Hartford and what the judge tells me. Now I am facing another warrant and am scared to death that I will end up in jail. Mark is a kind man in his 60's and he simply says, "I have seen this a million times and we will get you through this, but whatever you do…NEVER talk to the police. From this moment on, tell them to call me." He hands me his card, tells me to stay out of trouble, and that he will be in touch. The next day, I am fired from my job.

I will be arrested four more times before getting myself into rehab. My lawyer keeps filing a continuance in hope that I will get some help before having to get in front of the judge. The court would rather see you in a residential treatment center than in jail, especially if your only crimes are addiction-driven.

My back is against a wall. I have no job, no money, and no way to get pills. I have to come clean to my parents who are the only ones still speaking to me, albeit barely. I call my dad and choke out the words, "I am ready to get some help."

"We have been waiting a long time to hear you say that," he says. "We will take care of Hunter for as long as you need to be away." That night, I swallow the last of my stash, and the next day I am checking myself into the drug rehab that saves my life.

CHAPTER

3

Bring Your Own Soap

Your drug habit is a jealous lover that demands every ounce of you. It needs to come first and will destroy anything that dares to interfere.

One of the hardest parts of entering a life of recovery is accepting the fact that you are a drug addict. Does it define who you are as a person? Absolutely not. However, there is no denying that you have developed a relationship with a substance that has taken over your life. Every moment of every day has been consumed with thoughts and schemes to maintain your habit. *How many pills do I have? How will I get more? Where will I get the money to pay for my next bottle? Where could I steal some?* It becomes an obsession and takes your attention away from all the truly important things in your life.

Addiction has a life of its own and is happiest when you are giving it all your attention. It doesn't wait for an invitation to intrude on your life and destroy every relationship you have ever known; it simply invites itself in and refuses to leave.

But at some point, inevitably, your relationship with your addiction goes from love to hate. You start to see that the life of euphoria that it promised is no longer being delivered. It convinces you not to give up on it…just take *more* to get that sweet ecstasy you once had. And so, you do, but you quickly find out that you are chasing a ghost. The road to cloud nine has forked off and you find yourself traveling quickly to hell. The more you take, the further you drift into an abyss where all you see is darkness and despair.

Your once faithful love is now showing its true colors. The vibrant kaleidoscope that you once experienced is now nothing but black. And like a black hole, it's a constant and powerful pull into itself.

Your mind starts to obsess about an escape plan. A deep gash in the earth begs you to jump into the portal, promising you a safe refuge when you land. You will contemplate the offer, sitting at the edge and weighing your options. It's a simple choice: recovery, or death.

———————◇———————

It is 3 a.m. when I am dropped off at rehab. The withdrawal symptoms have started, so I am shaking uncontrollably. I am nauseous and barely able to lift my head. The intake nurse is not very sympathetic (no doubt affected by the continuous waves of negative vibes of one down-and-out junkie or alcoholic after another). She informs me more than once that if I cannot keep it together long enough to get through the questionnaire, then I will not be granted a bed. I manage to get through the intake, sign the paperwork, and promptly vomit all over her floor.

I'm now told to take a shower. I am shivering and have a headache so bad I am losing my vision. I politely ask if I can please skip the shower and just crawl into a bed. "Absolutely not!" scolds the nurse who has just finished cleaning up my vomit in her office. "Every resident that comes in must shower and put on the scrubs."

The shower is freezing cold, so I jump in and out as quickly as I can. "Try again," says Nurse Ratchet. "You have to wash your hair." I am now shaking so hard I cannot control my reflexes and feel every muscle in my body starting to cramp. I get through the shower and into the scrubs.

My hair still soaking wet, I am escorted into the detox center, where I will spend the next five days, sicker than I ever thought humanly possible. Withdrawal is horrific. Every cell in your body begs for relief. You have diarrhea and are vomiting at the same time. You are sweating one minute and freezing the next. Your muscles are cramping up and you are shaking uncontrollably. Your head hurts so much you can't rest on a pillow. You feel like your skin is crawling, and you would give anything to crawl out of it. It's a time of feeling crouched on that ledge where jumping to certain death seems appealing.

It's early on day six and a staff member enters the detox center and calls my name. He walks me out and to the room where I will be staying for the rest of my time in rehab. I am still very shaky and in desperate need of a shower. I am wearing the same scrubs they gave me when I entered the center five days earlier. I didn't know I was supposed to have packed a bag of clothes and toiletries (apparently, I skipped that part in the brochure). A large clock on the wall is the twin of one from my first-grade classroom. Void of aesthetics, it's only going to state the facts. It's straight-up eight o'clock.

A different guy is there to instruct me to go to the group meeting that is starting in a classroom down the hall. "Can I please take a shower first? I am disgusting," I beg the junior counselor.

"Do you have shampoo and soap?" he asks.

"I do not. Don't you supply those?"

He laughs. "This is rehab, not the Hilton. The residents need to bring their own supply of soap and shampoo."

"Good to know," I respond sarcastically. "I'll keep that in mind for the next time I visit. For now, can I please borrow some soap? Even hand soap will do. Please don't make me be around other people looking and smelling like this." He calls someone on his walkie-talkie.

And here I am, in the shower with a bottle of pink hand soap.

Now, it's my first group meeting and there are 14 residents, including me, all sitting in a circle. There are six women and eight men, ranging from early 20's to mid-30's. They are all in their regular street clothes, jeans and sweatshirts, and clearly had gotten themselves together before the meeting. I, on the other hand, sit in dirty clothes, have on no makeup, and my uncombed wet hair looks (as my mom would say) "like a rat's nest." I should be embarrassed, but I start to again feel so sick that I don't give a shit.

The lead counselor for this group (where I am the only new member) has everyone introduce themselves to me and tell me their sobriety day count. "Hi, I'm Lisa, addict, and I have seven days today," the first one speaks.

"Hi, Lisa!" the rest of the group responds in unison. Everyone follows suit and then it is my turn.

"Hi, I'm Deb, and I have been here for five days so I guess I have five days." I can barely think straight at this point. I have a splitting headache and every bone in my body aches. I am so uncomfortable sitting upright in this hard plastic chair. I am trying to pay attention, when all I want is to sleep. The counselor notices my fidgetiness and asks if I am okay. "Actually, no. I really don't feel well. Can I go back to my room and lie down?"

The girl across from me looks me up and down and spits out, "You can't go off on your own! You have to stay with the group." Then, to the leader, she continues, "If she doesn't feel good, she needs to go back to detox. She is a distraction to the group."

Wow, I think. *Thanks for the compassion.* The counselor looks at me and his face registers pity. He says I can go to my room and sleep for two hours. I'm told that if I can't join the group after that, I will have to go back to detox.

I crawl into the narrow bed with the plastic-wrapped pillow and fall fast asleep. I wake up to a counselor assistant banging on my door. I guess it's been two hours, but it feels like two minutes. I'm instructed to head to the cafeteria for lunch and then to resume the rest of the counseling sessions with the other residents. "When will I be able to make a phone call?" I ask. "I need to have my mom drop off some clothes and toiletries."

He looks at me and smirks. "Ask your counselor."

"I don't even know who my counselor is!" I snap. I'm a tornado of emotions inside a thick fog of detoxification. I just want to crawl back in the bed and sleep. Depression and anxiety are creeping in. I miss Hunter so much. Every time I think of him, my heart jumps up into my throat and I literally can't breathe for a second. He's been with my parents since the night I entered rehab. Being four, I know he is old enough to wonder where I am and why I haven't even called him. Guilt overwhelms me and I desperately want to hear his voice and assure him I am okay, even though I am far from it.

I meet the group at lunch and feel like I am the new kid in junior high school. The tables are filled, and conversation ensues between the individuals. I immediately notice the woman who was so nasty to me in the meeting. I swiftly pivot to a different area. There are four women at the table who introduce themselves as Tracy, Gina, Kerry, and Christine. They actually welcome me with hugs and tell me they are happy I am there. "You all seem so calm and normal. I feel like I have bugs crawling under my skin and can't sit still," I say.

"We have been here for a while. You'll start to feel better soon," Tracy says. This is her third time in rehab. She is court-ordered this time, after getting her third DUI. She has tried to stop drinking on her own for years but was never successful. She is hoping this time it will stick.

"I hope so, too," I tell her.

Gina asks me, "What's your story? Is this your first time in rehab?"

"This is my first time in an inpatient program," I answer. "I tried the outpatient program but was still using. I needed to go through detox, which I did, and now I am here. By the way, when will I find out who my counselor is? No one has given me any information about how this whole thing works."

"Our next session is at one and I think Jonathan is running it. You can ask him," says Christine.

I notice the time on the large wall clock is 12:45 and suddenly every person in the cafeteria starts to stand up and walk towards the back door. "Come on," Gina says, "time for a smoke break!"

"Oh, I don't smoke, so I'll wait here," I reply.

"Can't. We all have to stay together in a group no matter where we go." I look around and see 20 people staring at me and waiting for me to join them. The yard is fenced in with a few picnic tables and plastic chairs placed in a circle. Beyond the fence is marshland and lots of trees with leaves that are starting to turn yellow and orange in the cool October temperatures. The sky is bright blue without a cloud to be seen and I think, *this is nice...* This is the first time in almost four years that I am seeing the beauty of nature without being high, and for one quick moment, I feel grateful.

During the 15-minute smoke break, I am approached by just about everyone in the group as they say hello. One person keeps her distance—the same woman who snarled at me in the previous class when I asked to be excused so I could sleep. Her name is Angela and she clearly has taken issue with me. I am only 5'3" and she's even shorter, but what she lacks in height she makes up for in attitude. Wearing jeans, black leather boots, and a tank top which shows off her multiple tattoos, she keeps her chin slightly tilted up, sending a clear message that she is not to be messed with. I would learn later that she is finishing out her jail sentence for armed robbery. (Eighty percent of the rehab residents are doing the same, thanks to prison overcrowding.)

There is another thing that stands out to me about Angela; she is madly in love with Jim, whom she is sitting next to. Every time he speaks, her whole demeanor softens, and she frequently giggles, not laughs, but giggles when he shares a funny story. The minute anyone else leads the conversation or, to use meeting lingo, shares, she shifts in her seat and composes herself. Seeing that side of her immediately makes me feel less intimidated by her, realizing that she is just as vulnerable as the rest of us.

That's a huge aha you have in rehab, 12-Step meetings, or any group of recovering addicts—that is, that you have no idea how a person ended up in that room, but they are hurting and desperate, just like you.

When it comes my time to formally introduce myself and share the story of what brought me to rehab, I don't reveal much about myself that day, just the basics of having a pill addiction that had taken over my life. I notice that everyone is giving me their full attention, sans Angela who shifts around in her seat and makes loud sighs. I feel like I can read her mind. I know she is thinking that I am nothing more than a spoiled, rich white girl who was popping pills to get her daddy's attention.

I am being judged without her knowing anything about me, which is exactly what I have done all of my life to the nameless and faceless addicts I had never even met. That realization hits me like a ton of bricks. I look around the group; most of them have been in jail, prison, or been homeless at some point. Their road to addiction took away their children, family, and friends.

Just like me. At that moment I realize we are all the same. We might have come from different upbringings and socio-economic backgrounds, but we are all fighting the same disease. We are all ill-equipped to slay our dragons, and we've all seen our lives get scorched beyond recognition. None of us chose this outcome, but we all want desperately to turn ourselves around and break free from addiction. I realize quickly that I am no longer alone in my nightmare and that I never really was. There are so many people struggling with addiction and alcoholism, and we are all in this together.

———————◇———————

I am finally able to call my parents and talk to Hunter, who has been told I am not feeling well and am staying in a "place" that will make me well again. "What did he say when you told him that?" I ask my mom.

"He had a lot of questions about when he could see you and if the doctors will make you better," she says, "but we are keeping him busy and he seems fine. Trevor has been to visit him a few times. He is really worried about you. Said he had no idea you had a problem."

"Part of being an addict is learning how to cover it up," I say. "I guess I did a good job when it came to him. He has his own demons to battle…I really hope he can find a way out of it."

Hunter's voice is so sweet and innocent it makes my heart hurt. "Hi Mommy! Are you feeling better?" I feel like bursting into tears. The child's purity and goodness are like a blinding white light in stark comparison to my surroundings of addicts, convicts, and other desperate people trying to claw their way out of dark, dark places. My son's beautiful energy comes through the phone line, giving me strength to compose myself, for his sake.

"I am, honey, I am getting better every day," I say. "I miss you so much and can't wait to see you. I hear you're having a lot of fun with Gramma and Papa!"

"Yup. I am. Okay, bye!" And just like that, he is off. Hearing him and knowing he is doing just fine enables me to stop worrying about him and really start to focus on myself. Finally.

When I am in detox, I vaguely remember sitting at a table and listening to a few outsiders read from a book and talking about a higher power. I have no idea who they are or what they are talking about, nor do I care. It is on the second day of my rehab residency that the foggy memory starts to come back. Our group session is about NA (narcotics anonymous), and how the program works. We are handed a book and told we will read the first chapter which discusses Step One. At our next meeting, we will do the same, but read and discuss chapter two, then three...all the way through to the final step, twelve.

Our leader is Melissa (who, by the way, I finally find out is my counselor). Melissa explains to us (but mostly to me) that if we follow these steps and do the corresponding work, we will be free from our addiction and have a spiritual awakening that will change our lives. I believe her. *Sign me up!* I think.

We open the book and begin reading Step One:

"We admitted we were powerless over our addiction, that our lives had become unmanageable."

This one simple sentence describes my feelings to perfection. I have tried so hard, but I cannot stop taking drugs. I am powerless over them, and I have lost complete control over my life. Indeed, it has become unmanageable.

For the first time in years, I know that I am somewhere that I belong.

4

Stepping into the Steps

Life can be challenging, complicated, and painful. We all learn that, but how each person copes with that reality is different. Stress, repressed anger, fear…any unwelcome feeling can trigger a built-in need to "cope," and for me, there is no healthy, balanced response to those uncomfortable feelings.

To calm the noise in my head and settle the rage in my gut, I take a few Vicodin and before you know it, I don't care about any of it. I feel fine, thank you.

And that is how drugs become my coping crutch and what feels like my "lifesaver."

I have heard about Alcoholics Anonymous and have a general idea about it. I know that there are these "meetings" that people with drinking problems attend and, to my minimal knowledge, they somehow help each other stop drinking. Since alcohol isn't really my thing, meaning I only drink when I don't have anything else to numb myself with, I never think about going to a meeting or even finding out what they are all about. However, in rehab, you are required to attend both Alcoholics Anonymous (AA) and Narcotics Anonymous (NA) meetings every single day. I am so in the dark about addiction that I never even knew there was such a thing as NA. In AA and NA meetings, the goal is the same: To learn to live a healthy and productive life without the use of any mind-altering substance.

I should add that "mind-altering" or "numbing" does not always involve a "substance." There are support meetings for those addicted to overeating, sex, gambling, and more. One can become addicted to using all sorts of methods to escape from life.

The program is designed to not only abstain from using but to gain insight and understanding of the underlying issues that cause you to want to move through life void of any feelings. There are specific guidelines, or "steps" as we call them, to follow, which not only uncover certain behaviors and patterns we have, but help us to shift our way of thinking and/or behaving.

I've never really thought about my "patterns" of behavior before. Now I'm aware that time after time, I avoid conflict by acting sorry and submissive, followed by self-loathing for putting up with abusive behavior. The worse I feel about myself and my situation, the more eager I am to escape those painful feelings by self-medicating with pills.

The Twelve Steps are set up in a very specific way for good reason. If we don't follow each step, chances are we relapse. I have seen it happen more times than my heart wants to share.

The first three steps are what I like to call foundation steps. We are building a strong, concrete foundation for the rest of our recovery program.

In rehab, thankfully, I started taking these steps that millions of people before me have found crucial to recovery. Steps that countless people swear have saved their life. I include them here (with permission from NA) as they appear in NA literature, followed by my own description.

Later in this book, I go into my story, my deeply transformative journey through these twelve steps. I share my personal experience of working through the steps—it's different for everyone.

Beginning my stint in rehab is when I am introduced. I don't know yet what it would be like to complete them, but I trust that if they work so well for so many, they can work for me, too.

Here are the steps and a short description of what each is designed for.

Step One: *We admitted that we were powerless over our addiction, that our lives had become unmanageable.*

I'm someone who keeps a notebook to record my lies, as they are too numerous to remember or manage.

This step is about *honesty.*

The level of denial that comes with addiction is hard for onlookers to believe. No matter how much other people push (threaten with dire consequences) or pull (bribe with rewards), the addict must accept they have a problem before anything or anyone can actually help them.

The 12 Steps begin with an admission that you are powerless over drugs or alcohol. Once you admit that it's in control of you and not the other way around, you can get started.

Step Two: *We came to believe that a power greater than ourselves could restore us to sanity.*

A common definition of insanity is *doing the same things over and over and expecting different results.* By this definition, I am absolutely nuts. I would like to believe I could be restored to sanity. This step is about faith.

If you want God, or any Higher Power, to act on your behalf, it's imperative that you believe it can. I have tried on my own and failed many times to win the battle over my addiction. Taking this step means embracing the idea that it's possible, with the help of a Higher Power.

Step Three: *We made a decision to turn our will and our lives over to the care of God as we understood Him.*

Do I even know who God is? I haven't been in close contact, that's for sure. Does it matter? This step is about surrender. Oh, that's a hard one.

But it's only necessary to accept that there is some energy or entity in all of the universe that has a power outside of and bigger than one's own personal power. "God" may be different for everyone, and that's okay.

Step Four: *We made a searching and fearless moral inventory of ourselves.*

I am in a vicious cycle of pain, numbness, and denial, just like all addicts. Inside the cycle, there is no room for self-reflection. There is no time for soul-searching.

In the fourth step, we stop and take inventory, unearthing buried shameful behaviors, harms, and regrets. I'm advised, "You're only as sick as your secrets."

On the fourth step, we become unburdened and start to see the light and feel the freedom that is coming.

Step Five: *We admitted to God, to ourselves, and to another human being the exact nature of our wrongs.*

Admitting all my shit. Out loud. To another human being. Wow.

This is the "coming clean" step. We share our Step Four writings with a trusted individual (most commonly, a person's sponsor).

Step Five lets us tip the barrel of guilt and shame over and pour it out. Once empty, we can start filling it with the light, love, and joy that are possible in a clean and sober life.

Step Six: *We were entirely ready to have God remove all these defects of character.*

I must have some defects in my character since, over and over, I've acted in ways that harm myself and others and I have always been able to justify this.

This step is about acceptance. Blaming others and "life" has been a practice that serves us addicts well, inside the throes of addiction. Our low self-esteem drives our denial. We don't want to look at our "defects" so closely that we can identify them and ask for them to be removed, but we realize that being free of them *would* be amazing.

In order to move through this step, we have to be confident and certain that we are ready to let that shit go.

Step Seven: *We humbly asked Him to remove our shortcomings.*

This step is about humility. I can barely admit to having character defects, much less accept that I can't fix them. Nothing humbles me more. I do not want these flaws associated with me or anyone around me, but at this point, I am done beating myself up about how nasty I've behaved. I put the proverbial bat down and instead, get on my knees and lower my head.

Working through this step means we truly want our character flaws removed, leaving us able to fulfill our desire to be an honest, kind, loving human being who has *nothing to hide*.

Step Eight: *We Made a list of all persons we had harmed, and became willing to make amends to them all.*

I can handle this, I think. There's my dad, my mom, and Hunter (when he gets old enough). *Besides them, I haven't harmed anyone...* Wrong.

We must clean out all the cobwebs that are hiding in corners of rooms we've forgotten even exist. This can be an eye-opening step. The people that first come to mind are not going to be your whole list. But, this step is only a list, and a willingness. Nothing to take action on yet.

Step Nine: *We made direct amends to such people wherever possible, except when to do so would injure them or others.*

Do I have the courage? People in recovery find it, but only by standing on the accomplishment of previous steps and accepting help (like from a sponsor) and their Higher Power.

This step is preceded by eight important steps, and you'll have some traction on your road to recovery. I believe that this is the most freeing and healing step in recovery. Talk about soul-cleansing. The ninth step takes devotion, courage, and a long-term intention.

This step will free you from your past and allow you to change the trajectory of your life. A big part of this step is making amends to yourself, too. Forgiveness is freeing. This means healing, hope, and happiness will no longer be elusive.

Step Ten: *We continued to take personal inventory and when we were wrong, promptly admitted it.*

Chronic lying, like any ingrained habit, is tough to break. Even sober, my go-to behavior to avoid conflict is to lie and deny. The difference when you're in recovery and working the steps is that it gets easier to catch yourself. Then we can choose to "promptly admit" our mistakes and clean them up.

By the time we are on the tenth step, our level of awareness, including self-awareness, is so much more than ever before. This means we are able to maintain a clean and healthy lifestyle by regularly checking in with ourselves and being totally honest.

Step Eleven: *We sought through prayer and meditation to improve our conscious contact with God as we understood him, praying only for knowledge of His will for us and the power to carry that out.*

It's hard for me to confront this step. Not because I don't believe in God, or that I am not willing to live my life according to His will: It is because *I don't know how to pray or meditate.* I fumble through my prayers. I start with giving thanks, then have no idea what I am "supposed" to do.

In this step, we practice, most of all, simply making contact.

God just wants a relationship with us, that's all. He wants us to lay the burden of our lives on Him so we can be at peace. Through connecting with a Higher Power, we gain a new sense of purpose in our lives. Living with purpose is a great antidote to the poison of addictive thoughts and behaviors.

Step Twelve: *Having had a spiritual awakening as a result of these steps, we tried to carry this message to addicts, and to practice these principles in all of our affairs.*

To share the miracles resulting from recovering my life is a privilege. This step is what we naturally want to do after completing the first eleven steps. We have such positive things to offer others; things that can save their life. We can be a source of strength and hope, demonstrating that one can work their way out of the chains of addiction. Step Twelve shows up when we attend AA or NA meetings and share our life of honesty, openness, and faith. And it shows up everywhere we show up; you never know when a coworker, family member, neighbor, or friend needs to see and hear the message of hope that is unique to your experience, but relatable to theirs. Step twelve may one day even show up with you writing a book!

Step twelve is about service, and service is all about action. Time to apply everything you learned in AA and NA in your daily life, one day at a time, ongoingly. This way, you ensure a brighter future for yourself and you continue to be a beacon of hope for others.

———◇———

Working the 12 Steps takes time and energy, sometimes a lot of it. It took me just over a year to complete my Twelve Steps, only to start over again with the urging of my sponsor. In rehab, we focused only on the first three steps, ensuring that we would have solid ground beneath our feet before we started digging deep into our souls.

What I shared about the steps above is a very condensed version, not to be mistaken for the complete teachings as found in the "Big Book" of NA and AA, authored by Bill Wilson, which is the primary resource tool for all 12-Step recovery programs.

5

I'm Still Here

It is day four in rehab, and I am finally getting to know the cast of characters and what brings us all together. I am assigned a roommate whom I quickly come to adore and admire. Her name is Lucia, but everyone calls her "Little Lou" because she is a tiny little thing. I am only 5'3" and I tower over her. Little Lou has four grown children and three grandchildren who consider her the center of their universe. She is the glue that holds the family together through all their trials and tribulations. In addition to holding an impressive full-time executive assistant job, she is involved in several local nonprofits that support the less fortunate. My roommate has a very busy life, full of commitments. She also has a $500-a-day crack habit.

Little Lou and I become fast friends. This is not her first stay in rehab and I lean on her for answers to my many questions on what it is all about. "Honey, I had almost ten years of clean time before I relapsed a year ago and I can tell you two things with certainty," she says. "One, if you take the suggestions that this program offers— go to meetings, get a sponsor, work the steps—you WILL knock the monkey off of your shoulder and get your life back together. Two, if you don't, you will find yourself right back in an institution with everything you ever cared about gone. Including your child. It's that simple."

Prior to this "visit" to rehab, Little Lou had been very involved in her recovery program and her life was thriving—until she let her busy life steal time from her recovery. She stopped going to meetings on a regular basis and let go of commitments that had to do with NA. She neglects to stay connected to her sober friends and her sponsor, blaming her outside responsibilities for taking up her time. She "breaks the seal," as she describes it, and in no time, her disease is whispering in her ear, telling her she can handle life on her own.

On one particularly stressful day at work, she leaves for lunch, buys a rock of crack cocaine, and goes back to the office. When her boss finds her an hour later in the bathroom, smoking the aforementioned rock. she is immediately sent to the hospital and is now rooming with me at Riverland Rehab. Her family is onto her far earlier than this event and begs her to get help, taking away the privilege of spending time with her beloved grandchildren. She denies her drug use to everyone, and the resentments start, driving a bigger wedge between her family. She can no longer dispute it when she goes missing for a long weekend and is found by her daughter in a trap house. She has not seen or spoken to her family since then, which is close to eight months.

Back in group therapy, Lou continues to share her story with us, "I am so ashamed and embarrassed that I let my guard down against this disease. So many women have come to me for support and guidance over the years and now I feel like I let them down too. Why would they believe a word I said when I couldn't even listen to my own advice?"

Melissa, our counselor today, is quick to respond, "Lucia, that is your disease talking, not your recovery. Those negative feelings and thoughts are begging for you to block them out with a substance. Recognizing those dark thoughts and changing the narrative, allows us to move into our recovery." Lou seems to hear something in this message as she raises her chin and looks at Melissa instead of staring at the floor.

Melissa continues, "Let's remember to focus on the fact that you are here now, doing the right thing by not giving up or giving in. The attitude you're showing others is 'you can always get back up when you fall,' and that is nothing to be ashamed or embarrassed about."

We go around the room, each of us sharing about some trauma or situation that launched us into our addiction. "I was six years old when I took one of my sister's Ritalin," Christine shares. "I ran around like a lunatic for hours." She is looking up, like she's seeing an imaginary movie screen that is playing out the scene. "To this day, I can remember the rush I felt—it was like I discovered a superpower. I don't think I made the connection at the time that it was the Ritalin that was making me feel so good, but when I was eleven, I had my first alcohol drink, and those feelings came flooding back. I have chased that feeling every day since."

"I grew up around drugs my entire life," Jimmy tells us. "Both of my parents are addicts and have been in and out of jail for as long as I can remember. I started smoking weed and drinking when I was ten. No one noticed or cared what I was doing. I ended up in juvie for distributing heroin when I was in ninth grade and haven't been back home since." Jimmy pauses, as if hearing himself use the word "home" is painful. He takes a deep breath and slowly exhales. "I have spent the last fifteen years of my life in one institution or another, and I can't see that changing."

Donna tells us how she got hooked on prescription painkillers after suffering a back injury. "My back was fine after a week, but I pretended I was still in a lot of pain for several months so I could get more pills. When my husband figured out what I was doing, he called all of my doctors and told them not to write me any more prescriptions. I was so hooked and desperate that I left home and started buying heroin off the street." She chokes on the word "street." I can feel Donna feeling her past, her pain. She goes on, "I was homeless and prostituting myself for drugs. Apparently, I was attempting to go home one day when my daughter found me half-dead on the sidewalk near our house. An ambulance took me to the hospital. Now I'm here."

The stories of trauma go on and on—abuse, rape, molestation, violence, prostitution, sex trafficking, and blown-up careers and families. Day after day, we have counseling sessions individually and as a group, dredging up our deepest and darkest moments, bringing them into the light for all to see.

The words "We are only as sick as our secrets" hang on a banner in the cafeteria, along with other fellowship mottos: "Live and let live," "One Day at a Time," "Easy Does It," to name a few.

"What does that mean, exactly?" I ask Melissa about the "secrets" slogan. She turns the question back to me. "Let me ask you this… why would you keep a secret?"

"Because I don't want anyone to know about it."

"Why?" she presses.

"I guess because I am ashamed, or I have something that I don't want to be taken away from me."

"Right," she goes on, "you are holding onto something shameful because you are afraid of others finding out. In recovery, we must live in such a way that we don't have to hide anything. We live in the light, not in the darkness of shadows where secrets hide. If we hold onto negative behaviors or patterns, they will continue to cause us pain, and eventually, we will use drugs again to numb those feelings."

I think a lot about that motto; the cycle of addictive behavior, feeling shame about it, the secrets piling up until the pain "required" numbing…with addictive behavior.

A few days later, Kimmie shares the dark secret that has lived inside her like a caged monster for years. "I was fifteen when I started stealing painkillers from my family and friends' houses." She speaks softly, and I can hear the sweet sound of relief that comes with letting secrets out. "I would steal 'em, smash 'em, and snort 'em every day before school. I hated school and needed something to get me through the day. I did that for a few years before I got caught. I was kicked out of school and my house, so I moved in with my sister and my niece." She stops and looks at the counselor, Jacob, who encourages her to continue, letting her know she is in a safe place.

"My sister is fifteen years older than me," Kimmie says. "She moved out when I was two, so I never really knew her as a sister, more like an aunt. She had a daughter when she was eighteen, so my niece and I were only three years apart and super close. When I got kicked out of my house, Julie, my niece, begged my sister to let me stay with them. My sister, Lynn, was a single mom who worked full time and revolved her life around Julie, making sure she was always safe and taken care of, unlike how we grew up. I loved them both, but I can see how I also resented them—Lynn, for leaving me at the house of horror that we grew up in, and Julie, for having a life that I always wanted."

"Anyway," she continues, "I moved in, got a job as a waitress, and as far as Lynn knew, I stayed clean. She had made it very clear to me that under NO circumstances was I to drink or do drugs anywhere near Julie. I totally understood and abided by her rules. Well, sort of. I still got high, but never around my niece."

"One night, a guy came into the restaurant by himself and sat at one of my tables. He flirted with me, and I flirted back. Next thing you know, we are hanging out and getting high together, just weed, nothing hard. It was nice to have someone to chill with and he was really cool. I started staying at his place more and met his friends. So one night, I leave work after closing and head to his apartment where there are like fifteen people there, all smoking crack and meth!"

"'What the fuck is this?!!' I asked my man, and he just looks at me like it's no big deal," Kimmie says. "'It's just a little party, babe,' he says, 'come join the fun.' For a split second, I thought, I need to get out of here, but within a minute I was smoking a bowl of crack. I never went back to work or to my sister's house again. I just kept smoking anything I could get my hands on."

Kimmie starts to shudder, thinking back to this time leading up to the event that would change her forever.

"The relationship ended by him going to jail for armed robbery and me ending up on the streets selling myself for heroin, which was much cheaper than crack."

I feel my stomach tighten as I think how narrowly I escaped having to resort to that level of desperation. She continues, "I showed up at my sister's to steal some things from her to hock. I thought there would be no one home, but I was wrong. When my sister saw me coming, she opened the door just enough to scream at me to leave and never come back. Julie was with her, crying and begging her mom to get me some help.

I clearly needed it, but Lynn didn't want anything to do with me. I turned around and headed to a trap house."

Kimmie pauses, looking down at her hands in her lap, probably seeing that whole scene replay in her mind and again feeling how awful it felt. "About two weeks later, Julie, who had just gotten her license, found me on the street and begged me to get in her car. I told her no repeatedly, but she wouldn't leave, so I jumped in the front seat. 'I hate my mom,' she cried to me. 'She's such a bitch! She doesn't let me do anything and watches me like a hawk! I'm so sick of it!' I was coming off my last hit of dope and was beginning to feel sick. Before long, all I could think of was getting another bag to shoot up so I wouldn't be so sick. Julie kept going on and on and I just couldn't take it. I wanted to help her and talk with her about it, but without dope, I just couldn't. I asked her if she had any money on her and she handed me two twenties. I told her where to drive, bought a few bags and shot up. The next thing I remember, I woke up, looked over at Julie who had a needle hanging from her arm and foam coming out of her mouth." Kimmie began sobbing loudly, a river of tears streaming down her face.

Every single person in our group sits completely silent and still. No one knows what to say or do, but I can tell you without a doubt, that not one of us is focusing on our own head trash while she is sharing her traumatic event with us. One by one, we stand and go over to her. We all come together to give our support to her. We surround her with hugs and words of gratitude for sharing such a difficult memory with us, letting her know we love her and are proud of her.

"Kimmie," Jacob says softly as he takes her hands into his, "you have carried the heaviness of this trauma for years. I have watched you time after time try to save yourself, only to be pulled down again and again from the weight of the guilt and shame. This is the very first time you have shared your story and look around...all you are seeing is love. No condemnation. No judgement. Just love. It's time to let go of the weight of the past and open your heart and head to a beautiful future."

"I don't know how," Kimmie says, her face red but no longer streaming with tears.

"That's what we are here for," Jacob says.

The next few days for Kimmie are rough. She appears to be jittery and starts talking about leaving Riverland. She has relapse written all over her. I am still the new kid at Riverland, clueless as to what to do or say to her, so I keep my distance and watch her slowly disappear into herself. Truth be told, I am uncomfortable even looking at her in that state. I have felt those jitters and that anxiety many times and I know that the compulsive thoughts of using have invaded her brain. She fidgets in her chair, looking at the ground so not to make eye contact and biting her nails incessantly. The anxiety she is experiencing is palpable and is making me think of how nice it would be to have a strong drink and an oxy.

I am startled out of my daydream when Melissa, who is clearly noticing Kimmie's disconnect, asks us to all hold hands. She says we are going to say a prayer for our friend Kimmie and ask God to remove the compulsion to use from her. I don't think too much about the ask, seeing as we say the Serenity and the Our Father prayers several times a day. I look at Kimmie, wondering if she is going to just stand up and walk out because she clearly doesn't want any attention on her, but she just shrugs as if to say, "whatever."

We stand in a circle, holding hands. Melissa prays out loud for Kimmie: "Dear Heavenly Father, your daughter Kimmie is suffering and needs the power of your love. The darkness of her addiction is trying to extinguish the light of the Holy Spirit in her. She needs your protection from the devil who is fighting for her soul. Please send your archangels to shield her from the enemy and fight for her. God, we ask that the obsession to use drugs and alcohol leave our sister Kimmie. I ask this through Christ our Lord, Amen."

"Amen," we all say in unison, except for Kimmie who is now laying on the ground, with her hands in prayer position, crying uncontrollably.

I have never been part of anything like that before. I have only gone to church on Christmas for the past several years. I know how to ask God for help when I am in trouble or need something self-serving, but besides that, I have no idea about the Holy Spirit or the power of prayer—until that day.

When Kimmie is done crying, she suddenly starts laughing and cannot stop. We all look at Melissa as if wondering, "Is this what a mental breakdown looks like?" Melissa starts laughing too, as if it is an inside joke they aren't about to share with us. Finally, Kimmie wipes her eyes, sits up, and simply says, "I'm still here."

From that very moment on, there is no more talk or even a hint about leaving. She is fully engaged and seems to have been floating on air. She talks a lot about her niece and reminisces without pain about their times together growing up. She brushes her teeth and washes her hair and transforms into someone I am meeting for the first time.

No one asks her what happened to make her turn such a heavy page, but we all know something much bigger than us (as in humans) joined us during that day of prayer, fought for Kimmie's soul, and won.

A few days later, I ask Melissa what they had been laughing about. "The joy of watching God lift her up and pull her back from the edge of evil," she shares. "I have seen it happen a few times before in my life, and it is the purest and most beautiful thing you'll ever experience if you let it."

"What do you mean? What have you seen happen?" I ask.

Melissa looks me in the eyes, smiles, and asks me how often do I pray.

"After every meeting here we pray, so about seven times a day," I say.

"No, I mean get on your knees and have an open conversation with your Higher Power? Not asking for anything from Him, but just giving thanks for what you have and where you are?"

I am baffled. "Give thanks? Give thanks for what?" I snap back. "For my mess of a life? For being a drug addict? For not having a dime to my name? Or maybe I should give thanks for marrying a guy I thought loved me, but instead has so much contempt and hatred towards me that pulling me out of a car window by my hair gave him immense pleasure. What, exactly should I be thanking God for?!"

"All of it," she says. "Every single rotten thing that has ever happened to you, give thanks for it because without the pain and suffering, there can be no healing and ultimate joy. You can never know the glory of God unless you let Him in, and ask Him to release the pain of your past. You have tried to handle all of this on your own, but don't you see? It is so much bigger than you. It's bigger than all of us. But it's not too big for God. Lean into Him and let Him take it all away. HE didn't cause it, but He certainly can fix it."

I want so much to believe what she is saying, and that God is on my side, but I just can't see how that is possible. It would be another few weeks before I feel the hand of God touch and change my whole life.

6

You're Joking, Right?

"What is your biggest fear about living a sober life?" Little Lou asks one night as we lie awake waiting for sleep to come.

"Honestly?" I answer quietly, "I'm afraid that I won't be a good mom."

She laughs and says, "Because you were such a great mom, high on drugs all the time?"

"No, I definitely am not a good mom or a good example, but I have the energy to keep up with him and take him places and play with him. Without being high, I don't want to do anything. I'm exhausted all the time and can't imagine having to give my full attention to a rambunctious four-year-old," I admit.

This is a hard truth for me. As a single mother, I just cannot imagine taking care of everything without that boost of energy I get from Adderall and Vicodin. Getting through a day in rehab, where the only responsibility I have is to show up in recovery sessions, takes everything I have. How am I going to cook, clean, pay bills, do laundry, grocery shop, drive a car, and the million other things I am tasked with—not to mention entertain, feed, bathe, nurture, teach, and tend to the basic needs of a toddler? The very thought of it makes me want to give up. The progress I have made doesn't seem like enough "in the bank" to meet the looming pressures I anticipate. Is it possible to face and handle life's demands with no help from drugs? I frankly can't imagine it. Maybe for some people...

When I speak to my counselor later that day, I share my angst with her and ask how I am to handle everything. Once again, she throws a slogan at me: "One day at a time."

"Enough with the slogans! I'm serious!" I snap. "I honestly don't think I can get through an hour at a time being clean, let alone an entire day, so please give me some advice that will actually help!"

Melissa smiles and continues to share her wisdom. "Deb, 'one day at a time' carries a few different messages. The one I want you to focus on right now is that when we are new to recovery, we must focus only on the present. Looking towards the future and the 'what if's' will only get you overwhelmed and set up for a relapse. All you have is this very moment, this very day. As long as you continue to do the next right thing, you will conquer all of these unnecessary fears."

"The next right thing? What does that even mean?" I ask, still annoyed.

"It means," she says, "that when you are faced with a challenging life situation, you follow the principles you are being taught in recovery. For instance, you take time to evaluate the situation and ask for help and guidance from your sponsor or a trusted friend in the program. What you don't do is act on your first impulse, and you definitely don't self-medicate through it. You will have all the tools you need to get through difficult times. It's up to you if you use them."

I continue to become more and more terrified at the thought of leaving rehab. I have two days left at Riverland before my insurance cuts me loose, and I am filled with dread.

Eating their food is horrendous and living in an institutionalized setting is no treat, but I still would choose to stay longer if I was able. The outside world seems very daunting. I know I will be faced with legal and financial issues, not to mention having to explain myself to the people in my life who now know I have a drug problem. I feel the familiar pang of shame creep up again. Without drugs, rehab itself has become my escape for coping with the reality that I am an adult and a mother—and don't feel confident about fulfilling either role.

I know I am learning a lot about my disease and that addiction is not due to having no willpower or being weak-minded. Addiction has a biological basis. The way I process substances is different from a non-addict. The chemicals in my brain react in a certain way so that I am at higher risk than others for developing a substance use problem, regardless of how or where I was raised. The compulsion to feed my brain opioids becomes all that matters to me, placing everyone and everything in the backseat. I understand this, and I am certain that I will never use again, but I still prefer the safety of an atmosphere where I am safe from stress and shame.

"Okay, Deb," Melissa says, "today we will be starting the discharge process and I will tell you how I feel you have done here in the past 21 days. After that, I would like your feedback on my assessment and you can share with me anything you feel is relevant."

Part of me is really excited about this. I am proud of myself for coming this far in only three weeks. I have made it through the excruciating detox process and feel really engaged in learning about my disease and recovery. I have made a point of connecting with everyone in our group and love getting to know them and their life experiences. We are all so different, yet the same. I find it fascinating that no matter what race, religion, or nationality we are, or how and where we were raised, if you strip that all away, we are all the same. We are all born with a bright light inside of us and a beautiful soul, and as life propels us forward, we resolve to a way of living that takes us down and now we are trying to crush the same demon that was trying to take us out.

"Okay," I say with a smile, "let's do this!"

Melissa looks at the folder with my name and date of admittance on it and tosses it aside. "You have been here for almost three weeks, and I have not seen any real growth or proof that you are taking your disease seriously. I do not see you succeeding in recovery and I have a strong suspicion that you will relapse. Therefore, I am submitting to the judge that you did not adequately complete this program."

I am absolutely dumbfounded. "You're joking, right?"

"No, I am not," she replies, straight-faced.

"But I have done everything asked of me and been engaged in every single meeting! Christ! I know just about everything about everyone in our group because I am that invested in my recovery!" I snap at her.

"Exactly," Melissa continues, "you spend eighty percent of your time learning about everyone around you and focus less than twenty percent on yourself." She stops speaking for a minute as if to let that sink in.

"I watch you try to save just about everyone here from self-destruction," she goes on, "and all that does for you is make you vulnerable to relapse. You try to fix Gina's living situation to the point of offering her to come stay with you. Gina's living situation is not your responsibility and all that focus on everyone else is just a way for you to distract yourself from taking a closer look at your own issues. I've seen it happen a million times. I'd put money on the fact that you will end up back in here within a year."

Now I am enraged. "I can promise you that you will lose that bet. I will NEVER go back to using. And guess what? Getting to know the group and their life struggles has HELPED me to understand this disease and how to stay clean FAR more than any of the ridiculous 'activities' that you have us doing here! Do you really think that drawing pictures of ourselves is going to give us some special insight into our drug use? Or forcing us to sit through a movie about someone who wrecks their life by using drugs is going to make us suddenly understand our motives? No! We learn from each other! We learn by sharing our nightmares and fears with those who have the same ones!"

I get up to leave and she orders me to sit down. "Look," she starts, "I am not saying that you don't get the premise of addiction or understand how the program of recovery works. What I am saying is, if you had taken this time to dig deep into your motives and triggers, by the time you left here, you would have far more coping mechanisms and tools than you do right now. You think you are much farther along than you really are, and that false sense of strength is dangerous in early recovery."

I am still fuming. I shake my head and say flatly, "Fine, whatever. Can I go now?"

"Yes," she responds. "You have two more days here. Use them wisely."

I spend the rest of that afternoon keeping to myself and replaying in my mind the meeting between Melissa and me. The more I think about it, the angrier I get. It is bad enough that she doesn't recognize how great I am doing, but to send a letter of non-completion to the judge?! Her letter could jeopardize my case and send me to jail! All this suffering through detox and uprooting my life for rehab would be in vain.

"Hey, you, okay?" Little Lou asks as we sit at lunch with the rest of the women in our group.

"No. I'm not okay!" I go on to tell the girls all about my meeting with Melissa, ranting and raving over every word. "And then she said...!" And "How dare she?!" along with "She is literally the worst addiction counselor EVER!"

When I come up for a breath, I look around and notice that not one person at the table is looking at me. They all nervously stare down at the table or at each other.

"What?" I snap.

They all look at each other, and finally, Little Lou says, "Maybe she is right in some ways."

"WHAT?? How so??"

"Look at how angry you are. Just think about how you are handling this situation. You are told something that you don't want to hear, and now you develop a huge resentment...which, as you know, is only hurting you. You are wallowing in your anger all day instead of praying about the situation. You refuse to look at the part you play in the outcome and just want to blame Melissa for calling you out on your B.S."

Whoa. That stings. I sit for a minute taking in what she has just said. I trust Little Lou as my friend; she tells me the truth, regardless if it will hurt. She has many years in recovery and knows what behaviors will keep you sober and which ones will surely lead to a relapse. She is right on with her assessment of the situation.

My pride and ego are hurt by what Melissa has said and fear takes over when she tells me about the letter to the judge. Pride, ego, and fear are three very dangerous places to camp out in when you are an addict. Now, because of Little Lou's honesty, which I believe comes from a place of caring, I understand that my anger is my mask to hide my fear. I am afraid of living a clean and sober life. I am afraid of not being a good mom. I am afraid of going to jail.

I ask Melissa for another meeting, and she agrees. "I have had time to think about what you said, and I want to apologize for snapping at you. That was unkind and disrespectful."

Melissa sits across from me, looking almost annoyed, which in turn, annoys me, but I am not going to show my emotions again and risk another gut punch. But it comes anyway.

"Deb, do you see what you are doing here?"

"Yes, I am making an amends to you for my bad behavior," I answer.

"No, you are proving my point that you have not done an ounce of work on yourself. You are upset with me, and your feelings and reaction are valid. I share something with you that is not easy for you to hear. Now, instead of asking for my help to work out a plan of action to get you on solid footing in recovery, you apologize. Your focus is wanting me to think of you a certain way, in a positive light, not as someone who can't handle a hard truth."

I just stare at her, at a loss for words. She continues, "Your amends to me was just in hopes of making the uncomfortable situation disappear, so you don't have to deal with a conflict or risk having someone be upset with you. These types of situations will happen in life and if you don't use the tools of the program, chances are you will relapse."

She is right and now I am even more scared of leaving Riverland.

"Clearly, I am not ready to leave. How can I get my insurance to pay for more time?" I ask.

"We have already tried to get another week but have had no luck. They will only cover an outpatient relapse prevention program, which I highly recommend that you take advantage of. You'll need it and it will look good to the judge."

I start packing. One more day and I will be released into a world that looms now as an unfamiliar one. I cannot wait to see Hunter, give him a hug, and listen to all of the fun and exciting adventures he has had with his grandparents, but I am incredibly anxious about my competence as a single, clean and sober mom. I still feel the tug of the drugs and worry that I won't be strong enough to fight off the compulsion, especially on a difficult day, which I know will come.

The next morning comes quickly as I make my way to the last group session before being released. I suddenly become emotional. I have become so close to this group of people. The same people that a month ago, I would have never taken a second look at if I saw them on the street. I would have been nervous around them, fearing for my safety, and they would have seen me as an entitled snob from the burbs. Now, it is like we all share a special, unspoken connection. The certainty sets in that the likelihood of us seeing each other again is low, regardless of how close we are.

It is a statistical reality that some of us will relapse. Others will go back to jail to finish their court-appointed time. The ones who stay clean will most likely not be going to meetings close to where I am living; most do not have their own car or a way to get to a meeting any distance from where they live. Regardless, we hug and make promises to keep in touch. The one person I do keep in touch with for a short time is Little Lou. She keeps her promise of calling when she gets home, and we speak a few times a week for about a month before life's obligations keep us busy and we lose touch.

I walk out of the door to Riverland and won't return for another 10 years.

CHAPTER

7

S.O.B.E.R.
sonofabitch everything's real

I've never been away from my precious little boy for so long before, and I am excited and anxious to see him. (Later today, my first day out of rehab, I'll betray him once again.)

When I get home from Riverland, Hunter is still in his kindergarten class. I have about an hour and a half before I will surprise him at school and drive him home. I cannot wait to see him! I walk around our tiny apartment and take in everything for the first time with a clean and sober brain. My parents have been staying here with Hunter while I was away, so the place is spotless.

It feels surreal being here, knowing that a short time ago I was in this same physical space, but with a completely different mental state. I wonder if I can stay in this healthy frame of mind. I do hope so.

Before leaving rehab, I was given specific instructions by my counselor Melissa to do "90 in 90," which means going to 90 recovery meetings in 90 days. I also was to get a sponsor ASAP and start working the steps with them immediately.

I'm committed to staying clean, so I pull out the pamphlet listing of all the local meetings and see that there is an AA meeting at the church down the street that starts in 10 minutes. Perfect! Just enough time before grabbing Hunter at school.

I have never been inside this church before, so I wander the halls until I see an open door to a room full of people. There are about 40 people sitting at tables of 10, and in the front of the room stands a gentleman speaking to the crowd. Two things strike me as odd: one, the meeting has started before the time indicated in the brochure (which makes me late); and two, everyone in this meeting seems to be older, like over 70. I am unsure about going in because I am late and don't want to be rude, but then someone spots me and eagerly waves me in. *Okay,* I think, *I guess I'm going in.*

I quietly make my way to a table of women and assess that this must be a "speaker meeting." I've learned that 12-Step program meetings have a variety of formats, including one where a (clean and sober) member gets up and tells their story about their life before getting sober, what had them decide to get sober, and what their life is like now.

I can't help but notice that most of the people here are turning to look at me and nod or smile as a warm welcome. It's almost like they have never experienced a new person showing up at their meeting.

I smile back at everyone and mouth "thank you" to all those who mouth "So glad you're here!" I take a deep breath, ready to dive into my life in recovery outside of rehab. I politely smile as the lovely woman next to me scoots her seat closer and offers to share her book with me. "We are on Samuel 27," she whispers. *Oh, wow,* I think. The pieces begin to fall together. I am not at AA; I've wandered into a Bible study.

The speaker at the front of the room is not sharing his experience, strength, and hope in recovery, but is the church Reverend, sharing the story of David and the Philistines. *Oh no, how do I get myself out of this?* I am not about to just get up and rudely walk out, but I really want and need to find the AA meeting. It must be starting soon in another room.

I decide to wait it out and make the most out of the Bible study. I can't recall having ever opened a Bible and figure that it won't hurt. After a few minutes, the Reverand announces a break. I am immediately surrounded by several very sweet grandma types who keep telling me how nice it is to have a "young person" join them to learn the Scriptures. I don't know how to break it to them that I am there by mistake. I can't imagine admitting that I simply didn't read the small print in the Alcoholics Anonymous brochure and that, being a recovering drug addict, I really *need* to be in a different meeting.

Before I can make up an excuse to leave, the speaker approaches me and introduces himself as Reverend Wheeler. "It is nice to meet you sir, and I really do want to learn about the Bible someday, but I am afraid I walked into the wrong room. I am just out of rehab and meant to go to the AA meeting."

"Oh, is that right?" he responds with a gentle voice. "Come with me for a minute, if you will."

"Sure," I answer. *Who am I to say no to a man of God?*

Reverend Wheeler shows me to his office and asks me to take a seat. "Tell me about yourself and how you ended up in rehab," he says in such a kind way, I feel comfortable answering. I give him the abbreviated version because I really want to get to the AA meeting.

He asks if I have any children. "Yes, I have a son," I reply.

"What is his name?"

"Hunter…he's four."

I start to cry. I don't know why I've become so emotional. I think it's that talking to this man of God brings up my guilt and shame about what I've put Hunter through. I wonder how I'll ever be able to make amends to him. But I do know my heart and soul are committed to that.

The Reverend hands me a box of tissues. "What is the one thing that you think could keep you from remaining clean and sober today?"

I think about it for a minute and answer, "The craving. It is so strong all the time. I constantly must fight it, and it's exhausting. I worry I will give into it if I am not emotionally or mentally strong enough."

"I understand," he says, nodding. "We have a lot of alcoholism and addiction in my family. I can tell you that there are two things that I have seen save lives: Faith and meetings. I would love to know how you and Hunter are doing, so keep in touch." He stands up and walks to the doorway, points down the hall, and says, "The meeting is in that room."

Great. I am going to walk in late again.

Before I open the door to the 12-Step meeting, I hear a few women down the hall ask Reverend Wheeler where I am. He closes the door before I hear him answer.

The AA meeting is small, only five of us. After the meeting, a woman named Marilyn is the first one to introduce herself to me. "I want you to call me every day to let me know how you are doing," she says as she gives me a slip of paper with her phone number.

"Okay, I will," I tell her.

"And meet me here tomorrow night at six for the women's meeting."

"Will do." I walk out and jump into my car to head to Hunter's school to surprise him.

When I arrive at the school, I am shocked to see Trevor standing by the office. He has a bouquet of flowers. After hugging me, he says, "I wanted to give these to Hunter to surprise you with, but I blew it. Should have kept them in my car."

"Oh wow, that's so nice of you. Thank you," I say, cautiously. I am unsure if there is an alternative motive at play here. "I am so excited to see him. Does he have any idea I am home?"

"No," Trevor says, "I brought him to school today, so your parents had some time to pack up. He is going to flip when he sees you."

"How was he while I was gone?" I take the easy route instead of asking what I really want to know, which is how badly have I messed up this child, by him having an addict for a mom.

"He was great. Really." Trevor says. "He loved that your mom and dad stayed there and I am glad they did, too."

"Really? I thought for sure you would want to have him stay with you."

"I did at first, but then I realized it would be best for him to stay at home, so I just came to see him."

"Did he ask a lot of questions about me?" I feel desperate to get a glimpse inside Hunter's head. I want to know what to expect.

"Not really." He continues, "After we explained to him that you were away getting well, he never brought it up again."

I am happy to hear that Hunter wasn't in any emotional pain about my sudden disappearance, yet a little hurt that he didn't seem to even notice that I was gone. This is my addict mind in action.

The bell rings and the kindergarteners start marching down the hall with their teachers leading the way. I see him waiting in the bus line, holding onto his lunch box and laughing with his little friend about something. He first sees his dad. He runs to him, gives him a hug, and calls out to his classmate, "I guess I am not going on the bus today! See you tomorrow!"

I am standing next to Trevor, and my son doesn't even notice me until I bend down to his level and say, "Hi, Kiddo!" After his confusion lifts and his brain processes that it's me, he plows into my arms, and we both fall over. I feel tremendous relief, and my heart is about to burst with how much I love my son.

The three of us walk to my car and after I help Hunter buckle into his car seat, I hug Trevor and thank him for helping while I was gone. It's then I notice he is sweaty and shaking a bit. "Are you okay?" I ask. He looks sad. And he looks strung out.

"When I got the call from your dad telling me you were in rehab, I felt sick. I had no idea you were in so much trouble," he says. "I thought you had kicked it after your stay in the hospital."

"Oh, God no," I say. "I had another prescription in my hands the day I left the hospital."

"I am so sorry." He's choking up, and I know he wants to have a longer conversation, but I don't have it in me. Hunter announces that he is hungry, giving me a quick out.

I turn to get in my car as I say to Trevor, "It's okay. I am going to be okay." *But am I?*

I am cautious about Trevor. He is being kind to me, so I must wonder what's up. My mom tells me how distressed he was when he found out I was in rehab. He called Hunter every day and often came to visit him. Of course, I think he is setting the stage to fight me for full custody, but luckily, that request never comes. I will soon find out why.

By the time Hunter and I get to the apartment, I feel exhausted. I've been out of rehab for less than three hours and so much has been happening—Bible study, meeting the Reverand, the AA meeting, and being surprised by Trevor instead of being the surprise for Hunter. Reuniting with Hunter was overwhelmingly sweet; seeing Trevor in bad shape was disturbing. What an avalanche of emotions!

I make Hunter his favorite mac-and-cheese and then lie down on the couch. I have a tremendous need to sleep. When Hunter finishes, he comes over to me and asks if I need a nap. I open my arms, and he snuggles in. "I think I do need a nap," I say. "I'm still not feeling all better, and sleep will help me to heal. Will you take a nap with me?" Within minutes we are both sound asleep.

I wake up a few hours later to find Hunter sitting on the floor, watching a cartoon on TV. It takes me a minute to put together in my mind where I am. I wish I could say that my heart is full of love and gratitude at this moment, knowing I am back home with the only thing that matters to me, but as I become more aware of my surroundings, panic and anxiety hit me like a sledgehammer.

It feels like rehab was just a dream and I never left this nightmare. My body aches. Yes, withdrawals are still punishing me. I feel a migraine coming on. I lie here, frozen, my mind racing. *I can't do this.*

My mind is a swirl of mud. I review all the legal and financial trouble I have gotten into. I replay the many messes I've made with my family and friends. How will I ever face anyone again? How can I possibly repay my debts? How am I going to raise a child as a single mother? How am I going to get a job that will support us? On and on, the daunting thoughts pour over me, and I'm feeling panicked like I was literally trapped under a mudslide. I am 34 years old and starting my life over with less than zero, both financially and spiritually. I feel utterly defeated.

Wait! I remember—I have a hidden stash! My second-choice painkillers, not nearly as strong as Percocet, would still work to take the edge off. I quietly slither off the couch so as not to disturb Hunter, who is in front of the TV, lost in a fantasy world of his own. I tip-toe upstairs. Behind the bed, under the mattress, and through the closet I frantically search. My heart is pounding as I anticipate the relief of ingesting that little, white pill of happiness.

Damn! Where did I put those mother's little helpers? I know I hid a few here and a few there, in spots that no one would think to look—taped under the dresser drawer, in the pocket of a jacket I no longer wear, in an old purse that sits far back in my closet. Checking…but nothing!

Digging like a dog, down on my hands and knees in the closet, I freeze as I hear a soft voice. "Mommy? What are you looking for?"

"Hi honey, I didn't hear you come upstairs. I thought I had some cash hidden somewhere. I was going to take you to McDonalds for dinner," I lie to his face.

"Gramma cleaned your room when you were gone, so maybe she knows where it is."

Oh shit. My mother is notorious for her cleaning and would not leave one stone unturned, especially if she knew what to look for. My stash is gone, and I'm screwed.

"You're probably right. Hey, why don't you finish your show and I'll call Gramma."

Hunter heads downstairs. I feel sick with shame. I fall onto the floor, sobbing. I cannot believe how quickly my mind pivoted from recovery to addiction mode. The very second I thought I could use, everything that I just learned from rehab went out the window and there was no turning back. The beast had sensed my weakness and had come stark-raving alive. I'm heading backward in my recovery journey, just when I thought I was on a good path.

Yet, there is a flicker of light inside of me that refuses to be extinguished. As much as I will it to leave, so that I could only feel the familiar darkness, it refuses to do so. I reach for my phone and call Marilyn.

"Hi Deb!" she greets me. "I am so glad you called!"

"I'm a mess, and I need some help." I share what I had just been doing.

"Well, you did the right thing by calling me," she assures me. "You are brand new in recovery and this is your first day home from rehab, so of course it's going to be tough. Here is my advice to you…take it easy. Give yourself permission to not do anything but heal. Watch a movie or TV all day. Just get through the day without using."

"But I have a four-year-old that I must feed and entertain, so staying on the couch all day won't work. Plus, I am obsessing about using and I worry that if I don't keep busy, those thoughts will get the best of me."

"Okay, then, take baby steps," she says. "Every day go for a walk with your son to get out of the house. Start with a short walk and every day, add another ten minutes. And get to at least one meeting every day. Just get through *one day at a time.*"

Welp, there it is. Another slogan for me to choke on.

I hang up the phone and put my head in my hands, too emotionally and physically spent to cry. It hasn't been eight hours since I left Riverland and I am already falling apart. I can feel the fight inside of me brewing, the beast clawing its way around, hell-bent on extinguishing that small light of hope.

My addict brain tells me I only have two options: There is an easy way to get through my days (floating around with the help of mind-altering substances), or the hard way (trudging through each minute feeling like I am stuck in quicksand with a ball and chain attached to my ankle). This either/or, black-or-white thinking is a lie. I haven't learned that yet.

I know I have to make a choice every day…every hour…every moment. What will I give my energy to? On this day, the light wins. But only because I don't have the money or the means to feed the beast.

"Come on, Kiddo, we are going for a walk."

Hunter looks up at me. "How come?"

"Because," I answer, "we have been inside all afternoon, and we need to get some fresh air."

He still looks confused, like some unfamiliar entity has taken over his mother. I am never one to just "take a walk" for no necessary purpose, so this idea baffles him. He knows my time is usually spent driving around (from pharmacy to pharmacy) or staying inside (avoiding the possibility of running into another human being).

As he is putting on his coat, it occurs to me that there is a good chance of someone in our small neighborhood seeing me. I am not ready to face anyone or, God forbid, have a conversation of any kind.

"I have an idea," I say. "Let's drive someplace and take a walk instead of walking around our boring neighborhood. We can go exploring."

His little face lights up. "Let's go to the cement terry!!"

"The cement what?"

"The cement terry!" he keeps insisting.

All I can think of is perhaps my parents took him to a construction site while I was away, and he saw them pouring cement. I ask if Papa took him there. He nods yes.

"Oh, okay. Do you remember how to get there?" Dumb question.

He looks at me as if to say, "How could I possibly know that? I can't even see out the back window, let alone give you directions to the nearest construction site!"

"Never mind, I'll call Gramma to find out." I call my mom and ask her about the location of the before-mentioned "cement terry" and she is baffled as well.

"George?" she yells, "did you take Hunter to see a cement truck while we were at Deb's?"

"No."

I look at Hunter and ask, "Honey, are you sure Papa took you to see a cement truck?"

Frustrated, he says, "A cement terry! Not a truck!"

I hear my mother start laughing and then she shares with me that he and Papa had taken walks through the old cemetery down the road.

"A cemetery!? Why would dad take him there?" I am flabbergasted.

"They ended up there on one of their walks."

My dad chimes in, "I would read him the headstones and we would make up stories about the dead people's lives. He loved it."

Oh great.

So off we go to a cemetery where the headstones are so old that it is nearly impossible to read the inscriptions. It is a cold, grey day in November and I am in no frame of mind to wander around a depressing plot of land that is home to skeletons and ghosts, but Hunter is in his glory, running around, showing me the different headstones, and telling me the stories of their lives (made-up of course).

It feels good to be outside, breathing in cold, refreshing air, even if it is cemetery air, and for a split second, for a minuscule flicker of time, I feel okay. And then, it is gone.

When we leave the cemetery, it is close to dinner time, and I am coming undone. The emotions of the day and the constant anxiety of the beast coming for me are becoming more than I can handle. So, we go to McDonald's for dinner and by 7 p.m. we are both in bed.

As exhausted as I am, I cannot sleep. This is the first time in years that I am going to sleep without any chemical substance to guide me into my dreams. Even at Riverland, they were humane enough to give us Seroquel to sleep. My sleep is restless and by the time the alarm goes off, I am certain I didn't get a full hour of sleep. I envision the day in front of me and know it will take a miracle to get me through it.

Something clicks in my mind and out loud, I pray the Serenity Prayer: "God grant me the serenity to accept the things I cannot change, courage to change the things I can, and the wisdom to know the difference."

CHAPTER
8

The Power of Prayer

"God will take care of the rest." Oh, how I want to believe those words from the pastor. *I mean, he would know, right?*

My life consists of doing the bare minimum. My brain is still attempting to rewire itself and create the dopamine and serotonin that the drugs have been producing for years. It's a physically and mentally painful process to go through, and I know I am just starting.

I'm told to be gentle with myself. If you think about how you'd care for someone who is recovering from a grave illness and is still fragile, that's a good context for self-care when in recovery. Taking on too much can be overwhelming, and stress is the enemy of sobriety.

My sole priorities are taking care of Hunter and going to 12-Step meetings at the Congregation Church where I initially wandered into the Bible study class.

One Wednesday night, I arrive at the women's meeting early so that Hunter can play in the playground outside of the church before the meeting starts. I am pushing him on the swing when I see Reverend Wheeler walking towards us. It has been a month since I met him, and I am certain he won't remember me, so I am surprised to hear him say hello to me and Hunter, remembering both of our names.

"I've been wondering how you two have been doing," he says with a warm smile.

"We are doing well," I reply, "just taking everything slowly, you know…one day at a time."

He laughs and says, "There is a reason for each one of those slogans. They will all make sense to you soon enough. Just stay abstinent and do the work that is asked of you in the program. God will take care of the rest."

"Is it really that easy?" I ask, hoping. "I desperately want to believe that, but I can't see how God will be able to, or even want to, clean up the gigantic mess that I have made of my life."

"Let me ask you this…" he says. "How have your cravings been since we last spoke?"

I think about it for a minute. I am uncomfortable in every way. My bones ache, and I have massive headaches daily. My mind constantly flip-flops from gripping anxiety to major depression. I feel like I want to crawl out of my skin and hate everything about myself.

Yet—have I thought about taking a pill to dissolve all those feelings? Have I felt the familiar physical and emotional craving for Oxys that seductively called to me for years? The answer, miraculously, is "no." I share these thoughts with the pastor.

He smiles and says, "Good, that's what we prayed for in the Bible study that first day you came."

Whoa. I have to let that sink in for a minute. Did God really answer a prayer said for me and take away the insidious cravings that had gripped me for years, causing a mad cycle of addiction?

"You did?" I ask, still trying to make sense of it.

"Of course," he responds, "we always pray for the sick and suffering, and you seemed to be both." Forty people stood together, held hands, and asked God to intervene on my behalf. FORTY strangers! I will never again doubt the power of prayer or the intention of God to show me His infinite love, and this simple act of kindness, will carry me through the darkest days that are yet to come.

"I'm glad to see you're still going to meetings," he says. "Keep up the good work." He waves goodbye to Hunter and goes back into the church.

What must have seemed to him elementary literally changed my life.

In the fellowship of NA and AA (and in other 12-Step meetings), you hear a lot about the importance of having a Higher Power. This is applicable to people of all faiths and beliefs, as it gives hope that you really can be restored to sanity if you are open to the idea of looking outside yourself for help and support. Acknowledging a Higher Power also helps us to maintain humility, accepting that we cannot conquer addiction alone.

Many people call their Higher Power "God," and I am one of those people. My belief in God does not come from a religious upbringing. In fact, the only time our family goes to church is on Christmas. We attend Catholic services, and my memories of those visits do not inspire me at all to further seek more knowledge or understanding of God and Jesus. If anything, I am afraid of the mightiness of "people in the sky." Listening to the scriptures makes me feel inept for not understanding what is being read. The songs we sing make no sense to me, and I am embarrassed, trying to keep up with the verses.

Another reason I feel so disconnected from the church is the people—looking around, I see everyone very dressed up, Bible in hand, paying close attention to every word that the Priest speaks. They seem to know exactly what he is talking about and relish every word.

Sit. Stand. Kneel. Sit. Stand. Kneel. Over and over. Everyone except for me seems to know exactly what is expected of them, and I walk out of church feeling small, like someone who has missed an important life message that everyone else received. Regardless of the way I feel in church, I always believe that God is in Heaven looking over us—I just don't understand that He is looking after me.

I eventually pick up on the idea that you can pray to God for help. For years I pray for His help. I pray to Him when I need a passing grade in school. I pray to Him for a husband. I pray that we get the house we put a bid in on. I pray for Him to bless me with a baby. I pray to Him to get me out of trouble (many times). My list of things I want from Him is endless, and the more I feel my prayers are answered, the more I want.

Back during college, I prayed plenty. Yes, I received a passing grade so I could graduate and never look back, but honestly, it would have behooved me to retake a class or two so that I could actually *learn* something and start a career in my major. I prayed for a husband, and yes, I found someone to marry, but in the end, we both knew we were never meant to be.

I begged and pleaded nonstop for years to be blessed with a baby, but the journey to finally conceive was really, really tough. Not once have I ever simply prayed and asked that His will be done. Not. Once. My prayers are always asking for something I want, or begging to get away from something I don't want. I never considered that maybe God knows what would be best for me and that relaying to Him my urges and wants is not the same as being a humble child of God.

In the fellowship of recovery, I learn very quickly the importance of building and sustaining a relationship with God. For me, this journey has nothing to do with going to church or reading the Bible. It starts with me surrendering myself to Him and humbly asking Him to direct me in life.

I begin to let go of my attempts to control my life. I close my eyes and imagine the majestic power in the sky—clearly a power greater than myself. A power to trust that will gently guide me through my life and keep me on the right path.

I am very much aware that this way of thinking is unimaginable for many people. The thought of giving up control of their lives to some entity they cannot see or touch may seem ludicrous and foolish. I have and always will respect other people's feelings and thoughts about this subject, but all I can tell you is what my personal experience was and is when it comes to believing in something intangible.

I missed a step in my early development—that is, how to be discerning and make good decisions for myself. Throughout my life, I was surrounded by strong, intelligent, dominant people whom I trusted implicitly. Very few life decisions were made without the advice and guidance of these figures, and I learned from an early age that when I made a life choice on my own, it was often a bad one. Instead of being taught that we can learn from our mistakes, I learned not to trust my innate decision-making ability. Making a mistake was unacceptable and therefore, I became comfortable having someone else make decisions for me.

Whether it was my parents, brothers, boyfriends, girlfriends, or later, my husband, I never made a decision without input…not just input, but firm advice and direction. Anything from what style of clothes to buy or what college to attend, I felt incapable of choosing on my own. I knew I could be impulsive, and I needed a clear head around me to weigh pros and cons and basically tell me what to do.

I thought by the time I was married and starting a family my confidence would have improved, but it only got worse. My husband was the type that was all too agreeable to be the director in our family. I became overly reliant on him for validation. When I started to see his negative alter ego appear, I was even more certain that I was incapable of seeing the truth in any person or situation. How was it that the man I had been absolutely convinced loved me and would protect me from pain in this world was the very one inflicting it upon me? How, exactly, did I miss all the important signs?

Now, I have no idea what is in store for me, but what I do know, without a doubt, is that whatever comes my way, I will not only survive, but I will be okay. There is no factual reason behind my knowing, it just is. And this wondrous, innate feeling that develops the minute I turn my will and life over to God, I come to find out, is called faith. My faith sustains me and keeps me calm in the face of the devil many times in my life.

At the meeting this evening, I share with the group the conversation I had with the Reverend. When I finish, there is silence and tears. For some of the women in the meeting, they have never experienced the power of prayer, or even believed in it. What I share with them is, in their minds, miraculous. I agree. To me, having the cravings and compulsion to use be lifted so quickly after so many years of fighting against it, is nothing short of a miracle.

I do not need convincing as to the power of my God. I experience it and continue to every day that I remain clean and sober. I share that experience often at meetings and with every sponsee I work with. Whether they believe in God or don't, I tell them about the power of prayer and how it saves me and shifts the trajectory of my life. Some are moved by it to the point of having prayer as part of their daily practices and others are not. Either way, I respect and honor their choices. I am not here to try to change anyone or their beliefs. I am simply sharing how I stay abstinent from drugs and alcohol, and a BIG part of that is daily prayers.

Wow, I have learned a lot about what prayer actually is. I'm not sure what you'd call what I used to do, but it was more akin to a child begging to have their way than a conversation in which to *listen* with an intention to discern God's way. I recall a time when I was in college, found myself in big trouble of my own making, and cried out to God in desperation. Desperation to have things work out MY way, that is.

I think back. It's my third year of college, first semester at a new school. I have just met the one substance that made my heart nearly explode (both literally and figuratively) and that true love is named *cocaine.* The feeling of a stimulant hitting my mellow brain is an awakening I have never dreamed was possible. The fog lifts, the depression disappears. I am finally able to see and feel everything around me. I am wide awake and completely alert. High on cocaine, I tune in to my own passions and enthusiasm. I want to learn everything about all life has to offer. I am happy and outgoing, but also completely in control of my words and actions, unlike when I've been drunk and saying God knows what to God knows who. At last, I have found my soul mate and have no intention of ever ending this beautiful relationship.

Although I know this school will be more academically challenging for me, I am determined to graduate in two years with a transcript that will be my ticket to a graduate school of my choice.

My cocaine-riddled mind has other plans for me. Our Winter break is three weeks long, and I manage to hold it together for the first two, but when New Year's Eve arrives, all bets are off.

My friends and I are at a party where the alcohol is flowing and the cocaine is plentiful. I get so high that even after going back to my parent's house, I stay up for two days, not sleeping or eating. Exhausted, but sleep will not come. On day three, I finally sleep.

My crash is so hard, I am in a deep sleep that won't let up. I am due back at school in two days, but can only get out of bed long enough to hit the bathroom. Packing up and driving to school is out of the question. My parents are concerned that I may be seriously ill, but I tell them I have strep throat and just need to rest.

Time is up. Thankfully, my two roommates live close by and they get me and my car back to school. I'm still exhausted, but now that is eclipsed by anxiety. Cocaine created such an incredible dopamine high that now I am desperately worried that I may never feel that good again.

We arrive at the dorm. I climb under my bedcovers into darkness, and don't get up for any of my classes for another week. I'm now so far behind, I never recover and my grades are the worst I've ever had. The semester ends and summer break begins. A letter from the dean arrives, telling me I cannot come back for the fall semester and that I will only be welcome back in the spring under certain conditions.

The shame I feel makes me nauseous. The shock is surreal and the thought of telling my parents I have been kicked out of school is more than I can handle. I know they are paying a ridiculous amount of money for tuition so that I won't be burdened with student debt. I'm throwing their money away and slapping them in the face. I have failed them and myself, big time. I completely lose it.

I fall to my knees and start praying to God and begging him to get me out of this mess.

Wayward teens, college drop-outs, young addicts…people assume there must have been some kind of traumatic event in their childhood that paved the way to acting out as an attempt to cope. Sometimes, but not this time. Not in my childhood.

My dad had worked hard to provide for his family, at first working for an employer and then opening his own business. When my two older twin brothers and I were young, my dad was busy getting his business off the ground and our mom stayed at home raising us kids. We ate dinner as a family every night, had a comfortable, safe home, and wanted for nothing. There was nothing dysfunctional or abnormal about my childhood, just the opposite.

My grandparents lived two houses away from us, so there was always a steady flow of family and friends coming through our house. There was no fighting or drama between family members that I ever knew of, and although my dad enjoyed his nightly one shot of Jack Daniels on the rocks every evening, alcohol was not something that I really took notice of.

My mom was the one who dealt with the brunt of our misbehaving, mainly the constant bickering and childish battles between me and my brothers. My mom really had her hands full with us, but I never remember her ever making us feel anything less than completely loved. She nurtured our hearts and minds and continues to do so.

I have nothing but love and respect for my parents, so having to tell them that I have been kicked out of school feels devastating. In angst, I wait for my mother to get home. I'll tell her and discuss how in the world to tell my father.

Never happens, but today, my dad gets home before my mother. I find out she won't return until much later, as she's out celebrating a friend's birthday. I can't hide my distress and he asks me what's wrong. "Nothing…it's just that I have been asked not to return to school."

"By whom?" he asks. I pick up on a hint of aggravation coming from him which causes me to burst into tears. In between the sobs, I manage to spill it out. (Part truth, part lie.) "I had such a hard time this semester catching up after being sick that my GPA is so low that they want me to take the semester off." I prepare myself for the inevitable frown and the "I am very disappointed" speech, but it never comes.

"Screw them!" he says. "You don't need college!"

Wait…what? Not at all the response I expected.

My father continues to rant about "what a rip-off college is these days" and then the most incredible thing happens; he tells me something about himself that I never knew and can hardly believe. His grades were so bad in college that the only way he was able to graduate was by painting his professor's house in exchange for a passing grade. I am flabbergasted! My successful, intelligent, charming father almost failed out of college?! The mood has changed, and suddenly, I feel safe and secure with my dad. And incredibly relieved. He continues to tell me outrageous tales of his time at college and I feel more connected with him than ever before. It's amazing.

We tell my mom together. I have no panic like I felt earlier. As she lets this setback sink in, my dad speaks his words of wisdom to me. "Honey, you don't need a college education to be successful, you just need to be a good bullshitter." I look confused, so he continues, "Take for example a career in sales. You can have a very successful career in sales, regardless of what you are selling, you just need to know your audience. Be agreeable, listen to what they are telling you and if you don't understand something, just pretend that you do. In other words, bullshit your way into or out of a situation and you'll be just fine."

My mother adamantly disagrees.

I beg the school to give me another try and they do (with a very tight rein). I never use cocaine again, and I go on to graduate from college with a Bachelor's degree in psychology.

———————◇———————

In the fellowship, it is suggested that we surround ourselves with people who have something we want—not material, but spiritual. For instance, I listen to some women in our group who have such grace and peace about them that I am drawn to them. Meanwhile, I definitely do not have inner peace and I am fumbling through the days like a bull in a china shop. I want what they have.

On the other hand, there are women who seem stuck in a negative, dark vortex and spend the majority of their time complaining about everyone and everything. They go back and forth between playing victim and martyr. Some of these women have several years of sobriety but seem to be still living in fear and judgment of themselves and others. I do NOT want what they have.

Note: Just abstaining from drugs or alcohol does not mean you have availed yourself of the full benefits of recovery, healing, and living a healthy life of joy and peace. That requires a different commitment, and for me, it means connecting with those who are living in that authentic, clean, sober, and peaceful way.

It is crystal clear to me what type of people I need to be around to be successful in my recovery. I know I have to get a sponsor soon and start working the steps, and I want to make sure I pick the right one. I am weeks out of rehab and have gone to dozens of meetings, but have not met a woman who I feel connected to, or maybe I am too afraid to ask. Either way, I know it is time and I ask God to intervene.

I meet my sponsor Kristen at the Wednesday night women's meeting. She marches right up to me before the meeting, smiles, and states, "Hi! I'm Kristen and I am going to be your sponsor!"

I am taken aback and respond by saying, "Oh, isn't there some kind of interview process or something?" I thought I would get to pick my sponsor, not visa versa.

She laughs and says, "No, Marilyn is my sponsor and she told me all about you. She recommended that I sponsor you and as you'll find out, we usually follow the suggestions of our sponsors."

I am thrilled. I know right away that she is the right fit for me. Kristen walks into a room and hugs every single person she comes in contact with, and they all receive a "Hi Honey! How are you?!" She is funny, kind, and warm. We are about the same age and she has two children, one a year older and one a year younger than Hunter. We become fast friends and I hang onto every word she speaks about sobriety and follow any instruction she gives. Her drug of choice was opioids as well, so we have a lot in common. Just like me, she reaches for alcohol to quiet her mind, but the pills bring her to her knees and eventually into the fellowship.

Through Kristen, I meet a group of women who come to be my closest friends and supporters. I go from hiding from every living soul to looking forward to entering a room full of addicts every night. I get to know each of them through the stories of their lives that they so graciously share with me. They open their hearts and share the darkest parts of their souls for no other reason than to show me I am more than my addiction. I am more than my past behaviors. I am more than my past choices. I can be, if I choose to, a woman of dignity and strength who no longer has to hide in the shadows.

With every meeting or conversation I have with another addict, the veil of shame starts to disintegrate. Working through the Steps with my sponsor's patient, caring guidance is invaluable. I can feel God's presence. Before long, I can see clearly what my life looks like if I choose to stay in recovery. It is a beautiful vision.

CHAPTER

9

Progress, Not Perfection

When I was at Riverland, we spent a lot of time talking about "The Steps" and the importance of "working" them. The 12-Step program for addressing addiction does mean there are twelve specific steps to follow and everyone starts at the same place, on Step One. Some people take months to work through them, others take years. Many don't stick with the process and complete all the steps. In 12-Step recovery, "It works if you work it!" is repeated countless times.

To someone new to recovery, this whole concept makes little sense. It seems that every other sentence out of someone's mouth is about the steps: "You need to get a sponsor and work the steps," or, "Once you start your step work, you'll feel better," or, (and this is my favorite when I'm feeling irritable), "Do a fourth step about that." At this point in my recovery, I can't find my way out of a paper bag, let alone understand the gravity of step work, so I just nod and say, "Thanks...I'll do that." Once again, I feel like I missed the most important day in class where the teacher shared the meaning of life with all the students, and I was out sick.

What is the secret to taking "steps" when you're advised to not have a set plan? No timeline, no checklist to follow so you'd know for sure when one step is complete and it would be time to move on. Everyone around me seems to know the answer, but no one wants to enlighten me. Just like back in rehab, everyone in meetings seems to have an understanding of step work and expects me to know this as well. I will never forget that feeling, and so now when I meet someone who is just coming into recovery (a "newcomer"),

I give them an idea of what to expect at meetings and decode some of our jargon ("fellowship language").

To explain the steps and why they are such an important part of recovery, I use the definition from *The Narcotics Anonymous Step Working Guides* which states that step work enables us "to engage in some concrete activity that will help us find more freedom from our addiction…" This way of thinking helps me to wrap my head around why the process of the steps is going to keep me clean and sober, while learning what caused me to self-medicate in the first place.

In Chapter 4, I gave a brief overview of the steps and what each one was designed for. In the following pages, I take you through my journey with the steps. Everyone's experience is unique and their own. Here is mine:

Step One: *We admitted that we were powerless over our addiction, that our lives had become unmanageable.*

Lie after lie…I know my life has become unmanageable. There is no doubt about that. I've lied to so many people, I literally kept a notebook where I wrote down who I spoke to and what I told them; what pharmacies I had filled prescriptions at, when, and under what name; how many warrants I had and in what towns (so I would remember not to drive in them); and many, many other lies in my tangled web of deceit, desperation, and shame.

My bank account is often overdrawn, and I am months behind in rent and car payments. I've been fired from my job and arrested multiple times. My lifelong friends are no longer speaking to me, and my behavior is causing a tremendous amount of stress and embarrassment to my family. My brother says he's glad that the police reports printed in the paper didn't include my maiden name, so no one would know I am his sister. I suffer from agonizing paranoia and anxiety. There are rumors I'm dying from cancer due to my extreme weight loss caused by taking so many amphetamines.

I can easily acknowledge that my life is unmanageable, but am I going to admit I am powerless? The answer, finally, is an unequivocal

YES! Many people struggle with the word *powerless* because they crave the feeling (illusion) of being in control. Powerless? That makes them admit to a failure of some kind, but I am not one of those people. I know that my addiction was calling the shots in my life and there is nothing I could do—on my own—to make it stop. Lord knows I tried, but the physical pain of withdrawal and the mental anguish of living life with a sober mind has been too much for me to bear. My disease is far more in control than I am, and it's easy to see I am powerless.

There are others who feel they have complete control over their lives while using, and cannot see where or how unmanageability and powerlessness come into play. Perhaps they are "functioning addicts," running a successful business. Some are prominent attorneys or physicians. They show up for work every day, provide for their families, and believe that as long as they show up for life, who cares if they are high all day? Does it really matter if they popped an Adderall before conducting brain surgery or an oxy before their big trial?

As one newcomer said, "I kept my house clean and I made dinner every night. While my kids were at school, I would go over to my friend's…we would trade pills to help each other stay supplied. Sometimes we'd smoke a joint together, but I was always back home before my kids got home. I told myself the pills and pot were necessary to help me be a calm and patient mom."

By all accounts, many addicts look like they have it together, but unmanageability hides deep inside. They are preoccupied with thoughts of how they will sustain their habit. They may be paranoid that someone is on to them. They are behaving in a way that is against their values—lying to their loved ones, stealing medications, or taking stupid risks by buying drugs off the street. These are all internal conflicts, which are controlled by the power of the addiction and are making their lives unmanageable.

And then the internal unmanageability seeps to the outside, showing us and those around us the true magnitude of our predicament. The mom in the example above has a meltdown one day when she's out of pills and can't reach her friend. Instead of waking up to how unmanageable her life has become, she leaves a raging voicemail for her friend and drives to a walk-in clinic, faking an injury. Her children come home from school to a locked door and empty house. She finally shows up 20 minutes later in a state of extreme frustration at her failure to get a prescription. Can you see how her life is only going to get worse until she *admits that she is powerless over her addiction, that her life has become unmanageable?*

We can be certain about one thing—without admitting that our addiction is ruling our lives, the foundation of our program will be on very unsteady ground, with the surety of collapse as we add the other 11 steps.

When working on Step One, I learn that it's not as simple as admitting I need help; I also have to be ready to *surrender.* I wave the white flag to my nemesis and admit defeat, wholeheartedly, without reservations. If I hold on to any reservations at all, I'll be setting myself up for failure. Having reservations means being unsure I'm an addict, therefore keeping a small window open for relapse. To surrender means I am no longer fighting my addiction with denial and rationalizations.

Step One...*check!*

Step Two: *We came to believe that a power greater than ourselves could restore us to sanity.*

For me to understand this step, I have to remind myself of the many times I have tried to battle my disease on my own and the brutal loss I suffered every time. I simply cannot stop on my own. The cravings are merciless and make me crazy. I behave in ways I never would, had I not been driven to feed my insatiable desire for drugs.

It is easy for me to see this is way bigger than I am. To survive, I must get out of my own way and surrender. I turn to prayer and admit to God that I need Him and all His grace to relieve me of the insanity and chaos I am feeling.

Some, when they begin Step Two, look to others in the fellowship as a power greater than themselves. They recognize the success these clean and sober folks have had in recovery and choose them to help them through, fully admitting they could no longer rely on themselves to stop the mad cycle of addiction.

Once I am able to let go and let others in to guide me, I feel a sense of peace. Before my NA meeting starts, I listen to the chatter of the group. Here, among strangers whose last names are seldom known, a camaraderie born of common experience feeds our hunger for hope. The quiet laughter of recognition can be heard during meetings when someone shares a story of an experience that we can all relate to. Knowing I am no longer alone physically, emotionally, and spiritually, gives me hope and optimism that I can and will recover. Committing to that belief, to that possibility, is everything.

I finally see the hand of hope and recovery reaching for me, right here, ready to pull me from my familiar surroundings of darkness and despair. To reach out and grip that helping hand, all I have to do is to be *willing to believe* that a power greater than myself can restore my sanity.

Step Two…*check!*

Step Three: *We made a decision to turn our will and our lives over to the care of God as we understood Him.*

Countless people put up walls when it comes to this step. "I am NOT going to turn my life over to anyone, especially a God I don't believe in!"

I can't say I blame them, and I certainly don't judge them. So many men and women become addicted to the numbing effects of drugs and alcohol because of unspeakable trauma they suffered in life—how could they be expected to believe in a loving God who allowed such atrocities to happen to them? It's a fair question to ask when you've experienced such pain.

However, if we don't focus so much on the word *God*, Step Three can be easier for some to digest. Think of it as turning your will over to the care of whatever you understand to be a Higher Power. I don't know anyone who doesn't accept that there is some energy or entity in all of the universe that has a power outside of and bigger than one's own personal power. "God" may be different to everyone, and that's okay.

I know lots of people in recovery who don't believe in God. One fellowship friend shares how she came to understand Step Three.

She told her sponsor she did not believe in God and was asked to describe some energy force that was real but certainly outside of her own power, and what came to her was "universal truth." To her, this is real and all-powerful, and she sees that she certainly didn't personally create it, manage it, or control it. That's an example of how "Higher Power" can be defined differently for each person. Even if someone does not feel a guiding and protective force when first in recovery, they come to sense it as they continue their journey.

I remember sitting on the floor in my kitchen, head in hands, anguishing over what I should make for lunch. Having to choose between a turkey sandwich or a grilled cheese was just too much. Prior to my addiction, of course I could make a simple decision like that, but after years of living in chaos where food was an afterthought, I simply could not process even simple choices. For too many years, my addiction was steering, speeding, turning— always driving my life, minute by minute. I'm still so new to this clean and sober life in recovery that I become overwhelmed if I know I have to choose chocolate or vanilla.

I know that sounds ridiculous, but that is the reality for me. And there is a gift in this: when I have the thought that there is something wrong with me, that my thinking is really off in some way, that's my cue to look up (to God). Once I made the decision to let God into my life, I had to trust He would guide me, helping me to be clear enough to make good choices. Since I surrendered to God's will as the guiding power in my life, I am starting to feel more confident in decision-making, whether about what to eat for lunch or what I will make of my life. I embrace this step, eager to have something loving and powerful care for me. This feels like helpful guidance; my addiction felt like destructive control.

Earlier, I relayed my experience about "accidentally" finding myself in the middle of a church's small group meeting and then being prayed for by them and their pastor. This prayer power, I believe with all my heart, resulted in significant life improvements for my son and me, starting with my craving for drugs disappearing. After my experience with that group prayer, I knew beyond a doubt that God existed in my life and He would care for me if I let Him.

Step Three…*check!*

Step Four: *We made a searching and fearless moral inventory of ourselves.*

When we are in our disease (i.e., actively abusing drugs, alcohol, or any crutch that we become insanely dependent on), we are in a vicious cycle of pain, numbness, and denial. When we are numbing ourselves through our drug of choice, we behave in ways that we would not have, had we not been under the influence. This leads us to feelings of shame, which in turn causes us pain and escalates the urge to numb ourselves. Step Four works by unloading those burdens of regret, shame, or harm that keep us weighted down and on edge about our secrets. "You're only as sick as your secrets," one long-time sober peer said.

I look at this step as a cleansing of my soul. Picture the area of your body from the bottom of your neck to the bottom of your stomach as a vessel, if you will, where we stuff our negative feelings like guilt, fear, shame, resentment, sadness, anger, depression, and so on. These feelings are heavy and dark as night. With the crazy logic of addiction, we are sure we have no choice but to lug them around with us day after day, stuffing more and more ugly thoughts and feelings on top of the ones that have been festering there for years.

Substances and behaviors that help us avoid looking at or dealing with these become necessary for survival. Survival of our addict self, that is. I thought my drugs were like best friends because they shielded me from reality, dulled my memories, and numbed my pain.

While under the influence, I felt free of that soul-eating pain, but every morning in an active addict's life is a jolt of realization that the heap of darkness is still there, only worse. In utter despair, we ask ourselves, *How will I ever feel good again?* The answer is in Step Four. This is the time we pour out that container and start the process of resolving each thing instead of stepping over it and around it.

We write down people, places, and things that we have a resentment towards. We admit our wrongdoings and acknowledge responsibility for the part we played in the wreckage. We begin to identify our character liabilities along with our assets, and when we are done, we come to know who we really are.

It can feel very scary to let loose those nightmarish things we've locked away. The program, your fellows in recovery, your sponsor, and your Higher Power are there to support you. You're not facing this alone. It helps to remember that our goal in this step is to find our true self, the bright spirit that is in our core. Over the years, we have buried that spirit with layers of unhealthy behavior which, in turn, has caused harm and shame. Working this step is like experiencing nature's rain washing away all the pain, and then the sun shines.

My sponsor, Kristen, gives me specific instructions on how to work through this step. I am to write down who or what I have a resentment toward, explain the situation, and identify what I've done to contribute to the resentment. For instance, one of the resentments I have is toward a childhood friend who I feel abandoned me when I needed her. This is what my resentment work looks like, in an abbreviated sense:

> *I have a resentment towards:*
>
> Jane
>
> *What happened to cause this resentment:*
>
> She stopped all communication with me the minute she found out I had a drug problem instead of trying to help.
>
> *How did this make me feel?*
>
> Hurt, abandoned, unloved, unworthy, embarrassed, ashamed.
>
> *What part did I play in this?*
>
> I made an assumption that she would know what to do to help me. She knows nothing about drug addiction, and yet I wanted her to stop everything she was doing to make me better. I was self-centered and selfish in my thinking.

The above is an abridged example from my fourth step work; however, just the act of writing down what I have been feeling about a certain situation helps me to identify my emotions and helps me to identify some of my character defects (insecure, self-centered, fearful).

There will be some resentments that one knows they had no part in—for instance, physical, emotional, or sexual abuse that was inflicted upon them, and they are right. However, that doesn't mean the resulting feelings of anger and resentment can't be owned and worked through. The goal of Step Four is to remove the negative and harmful thoughts and feelings that keep us from living a healthy and fulfilling life. In order for that to happen, we must acknowledge what plagues us so that we can let it go and start the healing process.

This step reveals to me certain patterns in my behavior that have kept me stuck in my addiction. Once a negative pattern is recognized, I can change that behavior and break the cycle. I can now address any negative feelings I carry or resentments toward others that I hold. I am unloading all the negative energy and emotions I've been harboring. Putting on paper anything that may keep me from moving forward is like cleaning off a window that has years of dirt and grime on it. I never realized the amount of sunshine that was waiting to shine through! On the fourth step, you start to see the light and feel the easy-breezy freedom that is coming.

Step Four…*check!*

Step Five: *We admitted to God, to ourselves, and to another human being the exact nature of our wrongs.*

This is the "coming clean" step in more ways than one. At this juncture, we share our Step Four writings with a trusted individual (most commonly, a person's sponsor).

Step Five lets us tip the barrel of guilt and shame over and pour it out. It's only when it is empty that we can start filling it with light, love, happiness, joy, and all the other beautiful feelings that our Creator wants us to feel and experience. Finally, after working through four previous steps, this is a true beginning for a new and amazing life ahead.

Most people dread exposing their dark secrets. They are uncomfortable having another person look at such intimate and cringe-worthy details. After all, we spent YEARS trying to cover up all the indecencies of our lives.

I remind myself that my sponsor has "heard it all before," but I still worry, *what will she think of me when she hears THAT? Will I be judged and condemned?* And THIS? *How can I admit that to her, to anyone, or even to God?* I can feel the shame swaddle me like a scratchy wool blanket.

I want to run and hide. But I know that unless I face my fears and buried secrets and talk about them, I will never be free—and I am desperate to be free. So here I sit, just me, my sponsor, and my pages and pages of fourth-step writings.

I am lucky to have Kristen. Even though I met her only three months ago, I know we share a lot of the same life experiences and tendencies. Many of our step-work meetings last hours more than expected because of the stories and ideas we feel free to share in the emotionally safe space we've created. We also share the same sense of humor, so it's not unusual for our meetings to get sidetracked with howling laughter.

Kristen is generous with her time, telling me we'll work through my fifth step for as long as it takes. She knows the importance of being free from the guilt and shame I've been carrying like a heavy sack of rotten potatoes. I've finally tired of bringing that sack with me everywhere I go, and I surely don't want to add anything to it. She provides what feels like a safe, nonjudgmental space, a clearing for me to empty out every dark secret. I can feel my burden lighten as we talk.

I begin telling her about a past situation that still haunts me. This is how it unfolded at the time:

I am running out of pills and of ways to get my hands on them. I remember that my neighbor across the street is undergoing cancer treatment (I've never met her but was told by another neighbor). I am certain she'd have some good pain meds. Without thinking twice, I make a batch of cookies and march across the street to show my kindness, caring, and support to my ill neighbor.

She answers the door, and I can immediately tell she is very sick. Her pale scalp has no hair, her eyes are dark, and she looks so frail, it's hard to believe she could stand to open the door. Despite her physical condition, she seems delighted to have a visitor.

"Hi, I'm Deb from across the street," I say with a warm smile. "I understand you are not feeling well, and I wondered if I could help you with anything."

"Oh my!" she responds. "How nice of you! My name is June." She waves me inside and instructs me to have a seat. I set the cookies on the coffee table in front of where she sits down.

"These look delicious," she says, looking at them. She's skin and bones. She's not at all interested in eating cookies and the sight of them is probably making her nauseous. Her cancer hasn't killed her grace.

I look around her little home, taking in all the clutter and disorder. So many trinkets and knick-knacks everywhere. Like a hawk, I'm scanning for only one target and that's a pill bottle. My heart leaps into my throat as I spy several next to her chair, my prey perched atop a stack of *Reader's Digests*. I'm super excited in anticipation of getting my hands on them.

"It's so nice of you to come by," June says, "I see your little boy playing outside and you watch him from your porch."

"Yes, I get nervous when he is playing in the front yard, so I make sure I can see him," I say.

"I don't blame you. People drive down our street far too fast."

"True. I am sorry to have heard you have cancer, June. That's so hard. May I ask what kind of cancer you have?" I asked with a caring, inquisitive voice.

"Lung cancer, stage four. I was diagnosed last year and been fighting ever since. It's been a tough road, but I know the good Lord will save me."

"Oh wow," I say. "My brother and mother have both had cancer, so I can understand how hard it is to undergo the treatments."

"Are they still with us?" June asks.

"Yes, thank God."

"Praise the Lord."

"How are you tolerating the treatment? Are you in a lot of pain?" I ask, my heart beating faster.

"No, not too much. I am grateful for that because I can't tolerate the pain meds they give me. They make me so nauseous!"

"Oh dear, that's not good." I am thinking, *This IS good. She won't miss them.*

I've chatted for half an hour and now it's time to make my move. I ask June—frail, sick June, barely able to walk—if she will please go get me a glass of water.

She looks at me a bit stunned, but she's too polite to say *no*. It takes her a minute or two to get up from her chair and another three to get into the kitchen. Once out of sight, I look over her eight bottles of pills and find the one I am looking for. Percocet 10/325. Bingo. The bottle is filled to the brim, so I take a handful, which amounts to fifteen pills. I don't want it to be noticeable, but I need enough to get me through the day.

June comes to the kitchen doorway holding my glass of water. I take it from her and help her back to her chair. No harm, no foul. We have another nice chat and I tell her I will be back tomorrow for another visit if she would like that. "Oh, yes, please. I would very much like that."

I end up stealing all of her pain meds over the next couple of weeks. I call her doctor's office on her behalf to get more. This scam lasts until I go to rehab. By the time I get out, June is in the hospital and never returns home.

I swore I would never tell anyone about this despicable ruse I pulled to get drugs, but here I am, spilling my guts to Kristen. I am deeply aware that in order for me to unload all the hidden heavy secrets inside, I must be rigorously honest and bring them into the light.

With my inner "container" now free from darkness and despair, I feel an overwhelming need to fill it again. The void feels unfamiliar and very uncomfortable. Thank God I am sober enough to realize I have a choice and do not have to resort to old behaviors. I know I need to find something good that will satisfy the emptiness, I just have no idea what. What I don't yet realize is that something is already making its way towards me to answer that calling and change my life forever.

Step Five…*check!*

Step Six: *We were entirely ready to have God remove all these defects of character.*

It is somewhat easy to write down all the people who wronged us and all the things that kept us down, but when you have been living with and feeling those emotions for so long, it can be difficult to truly let them go.

Oh sure, we tell ourselves we don't want to harbor negative feelings or continue blaming someone for hurting us, but those feelings have become familiar and comfortable over the years. Looking at the harms that have been done to us is always easier than having to look at ourselves, our issues, or our own ways we've harmed others.

Well, in order to move through this step, we have to be confident and certain that we are ready to let that shit go. Some of us will pray to have these feelings and thoughts removed, and they will be. Other times we have to continue to work on recognizing and addressing our negative behavior for months or years. Regardless of how long it takes, it is imperative to keep working through this step for the sake of staying clean and sober. For the sake of life.

Completing the fifth step in a thorough way, we see our character limitations as well as our positive attributes. We acknowledge any past behaviors that we have been holding onto in secrecy. Patterns of behavior come to the surface as we review our fourth step with our sponsor in the fifth step.

Step Six is when we come to terms with our character limitations that have kept us stuck in the cycle of an unhealthy lifestyle. Character defects or limitations are not horrible, intrusive, unacceptable traits; they are basic human qualities that have become inflated or distorted.

For example, having a healthy ego (mindset about yourself) is not a bad thing by any means; in fact, it is something I strive for on a daily basis. For me, that allows for a feeling of serenity, a sense of resilience, and a strong awareness of self. A person with an inflated ego may live with feelings of superiority or entitlement. This is not healthy and often causes detrimental behavior. In order to create a balance, we must first recognize when our ego is inflated and learn how to deflate it.

It can work the opposite way as well. Our egos can suffer from fears and insecurities, causing great pain and anxiety. When we start telling ourselves that we are worthless and unworthy, this is a sign that our ego is in an unhealthy state; our mindset is actually self-harming. Once we recognize where we are and become open to taking the proper steps to reach a healthy balance, we become willing to have God remove these character defects—and that is the premise of Step Six. This, of course, is the remedy that replaces using.

Everyone has character flaws. Mine include dishonesty, selfishness, impulsiveness, stubbornness, self-centered fear, anger issues, and jealousy, among others. Any character defect identified should not be despised because in some way it actually served to help us cope and survive the toughest challenges. Letting go of these would be impossible, in my opinion, without a commitment to recovery and the help of a Higher Power.

Step Six…*check!*

Step Seven: *We humbly asked Him to remove our shortcomings.*

Nothing humbles me more than admitting to having character defects. Even though I know "I'm only human," I would rather think of myself as being near-perfect and never being part of any problem that comes along in my life. Working Step Six knocks me right out of my make-believe world and forces me to take a good, hard look at my less-than-stellar traits. I see patterns of manipulation, self-centeredness, and dishonesty, to name a few.

I do not like having to own these. I do not want these flaws associated with me or anyone around me, but at this point, I am done beating myself up about how nasty I've behaved. I put the proverbial bat down and instead, get on my knees and lower my head.

I have seen how God worked in my life before, and I am confident He is listening to me when I *humbly* ask him to remove my shortcomings. I lay them all out for Him, every one of them (not that He isn't already aware!). I concede that I know this behavior is not part of His plan for my life and ask if He will please remove these flaws. I tell him I am ready to be the woman He created me to be. I want my character flaws removed, leaving me able to fulfill my commitment to be an honest, kind, loving human being who has *nothing to hide.*

I can feel His presence. Tears pour out of my eyes when, at the end of my conversation with Him, I feel a warm calmness surround me that I have never felt before in my entire life. I know, without a doubt, that no matter what life may throw at me, I will be just fine. I have the Holy Spirit to replace my character flaws, as long as I remain humble. And sober.

It is through Step Seven that we strip away all that has been holding us down and become willing to try a new, spiritual way of life. It feels like both surrender and victory at the same time.

Step Seven...*check!*

Step Eight: *We made a list of all persons we had harmed, and became willing to make amends to them all.*

My sponsor explains that my job here is to simply make a list and become *willing* to make amends. *I can handle this*, I think. Obviously, I will apologize to my mom and to my dad and to Hunter (when he is old enough). I hear the voice in my head, *besides them, I haven't harmed anyone...*

This is an eye-opening step for me. I start to see how wrong I am, thinking that only my parents and son have been affected. My addiction has touched so many people. It's like taking a helicopter ride to review the damage after a tornado. The wreckage spans far and wide.

I see and regret the anguish I put my close family through, but there are many others, including my ex-husband—this is a tough pill to swallow. Am I willing to make amends to them ALL?

I remind myself that, for this step, I only have to *be willing* to make amends. "Just be willing," I keep repeating.

Step Eight...*check!*

Step Nine: *We made direct amends to such people wherever possible, except when to do so would injure them or others.*

What I am learning at this point in my recovery is that the quickest way to relapse is to continue to harbor harmful feelings and thoughts inside. Certainly, guilt and remorse fall into that category for me. If I am going to maintain a life of sobriety, recovery, and sanity, I must face the demons of my past and do the right thing by the people I have hurt.

Telling someone that you are truly sorry for your actions that caused them pain or distress, physical, emotional, or spiritual, is the key that unlocks true healing, and for me, the portal to God.

My sponsor is so encouraging. I know I wouldn't be this far along in my step work without her. She assures me that this step will free me from the bondage of my past and allow me to change the trajectory of my life.

There will be some people, she warns, who are not ready to hear or accept my amends. Rather than disrupt my recovery, I will simply let them be, as everyone needs their own time to heal.

When my amends efforts are rejected, I keep going. I write a letter if someone refuses to see me in person, or if they are no longer alive. What is important is for me to identify each and every person and make my best attempt to apologize. I acknowledge and take responsibility for any negative effect my behavior had on them. I let them know that I now live a different, clean life.

I make amends to my parents first. Face to face, not through a letter. They both insist it is not necessary, that me staying clean is all they want and need. But that is not sufficient for me. This step is clear. I think I've made direct amends to them enough to consider this step complete, but I am making daily amends to them by being the good (and sober) person they raised me to be. This is how I stay healthy and avoid relapse. One day at a time.

I'm finding that some on my list are taking longer for me to work through—like Trevor. From the outside, anyone looking at how he treated me would never understand why I owe him an amends, since he was the one who delivered the blows. But, thanks to my recovery, I now understand that when I was using, I played a part in the chaos.

I may not have physically or emotionally hurt him, but I lied to his face countless times. As a drug addict, it didn't matter who I had to manipulate or lie to in order to help me feed my habit—not even my husband, the father of my child.

I make direct amends to him, and immediately feel better for having let go of the anger and hate. My yearning for recovery far outweighs my desire to hold onto a grudge.

I now understand his struggles and the disease he battles every minute of the day. I also come to recognize that the demons come from deep wounds, inflicted long before I came into his life. For me to hold onto past events does me no good and could very well cause me to relapse.

Of course, the recovery process and this step in particular are ways that you are making amends to yourself, too. By living clean, you are making what is sometimes called a "living amends." This is the most important amends, since no apologies to others matter if you aren't committed to living clean.

Step Nine...*check!*

Step Ten: *We continued to take personal inventory and when we were wrong, promptly admitted it.*

One of my biggest character defects is avoiding conflict by any means, even if it means lying. To avoid someone's disapproval or disagreement, I simply lie and deny. I must acknowledge my progress here. Thanks to me sticking with my recovery program, I am no longer a chronic liar.

But when I was new in recovery (only about 6 months clean) and had just started a new job, I fell into my old habit of lying. Here is how I fell off the wagon and landed in toxic mud:

I'm being trained by another girl in the office who seems super nice and cool. We spend lots of time talking about our lives, and I feel like she is becoming a good friend.

It's a small company, so not much goes unnoticed, like when the manager of the company and our department manager spend a lot of time together and openly flirt with each other. Both are married, so there is buzz around the office of an affair.

I keep my mouth shut and never participate in the gossip—until today. I see our manager come out of her boss's office looking disheveled, her face a little flushed. I ask if she is okay, to which she replies, "Never better," with a Cheshire cat grin across her face. I am a bit stunned. I run back to my cubicle and in a moment of weakness, share the encounter with my co-worker friend. Too juicy not to! We both laugh and carry on about how brazen and unprofessional they are. On and on we go about it, then return to our tasks at hand.

The next day, my manager calls me into her office. "Have you been spreading rumors about me?" She accuses me of gossiping about her and her boss. Shocked that my coworker has ratted me out and embarrassed that I have been caught behaving so badly, I simply deny it.

"No!" I stammer, "I haven't said a thing. I didn't even notice anything about you two." Without solid proof, she has no choice but to let me off with a stern warning to mind my own business.

All throughout the day, I have an awful twist in my gut. Yes, I am upset to find out my "friend" wasn't a friend at all, and I just got reamed out by my boss, but it is something more. Imagine a clean white rug and how a glob of mud would stand out on it. Before recovery, my "rug" was so muddy that one more glob (lie) would not have even shown up to me. But now I like my clean-feeling life. I am not willing to lose it. I lie awake at night, can't sleep.

This morning, I come into work and, first thing, I march into her office and say, "I owe you an amends. I lied to you yesterday. I absolutely said those things and I am so very sorry. It was wrong of me to gossip, and it is absolutely none of my business what happens in other people's lives."

She stands there completely silent, looking a little taken aback. Finally, she says, "Thank you for your honesty. I really admire that you had the guts to come forward and admit what you said. I am so sick of this place and the two-faced people here. I wish they would just straight up ask me if there was something they want to know."

I do not dare ask her and honestly, I really don't care. "Live and let live" is my new motto. We leave the conversation with even a better boss-employee relationship than before I made my mistake. I am relieved that I'm not fired. I feel great, in fact, that my courage to make amends paid off, just like the tenth step promises.

I know in my bones now that lying is no longer okay with ME. And I know that if I resort to telling a lie, I'll have to admit to it and clean it up. After a while, the agony of having to make amends will become much heavier than telling the truth to begin with.

By the time we get to this step, we know when we owe someone an amends. Your sober brain won't let you rest until you correct the wrong that was made, and eventually, you'll change that behavior without even realizing it. This is a spiritual awakening. The inner strength that begins to rebuild once you have a clean foundation feels great and is motivating.

Step Ten...*check!*

Step Eleven: *We sought through prayer and meditation to improve our conscious contact with God as we understood him, praying only for knowledge of His will for us and the power to carry that out.*

I struggle with this step for the longest time, not because I don't believe in God, or that I am not willing to live my life according to His will: It's because *I don't know how to pray or meditate.* I flounder through my prayers every time I try. It is easy to give thanks (and very important), but after that, I have no idea what I am doing. Do I have to memorize and say specific prayers that are already written? Should I be using words like "Thou" and "Sovereign"? What if I forget something important to ask Him? I picture God anxiously awaiting my prayer, only to have it end with a disappointed head shake from Him.

Meditation is out of reach for me, too. I mean, who can sit quietly and clear their minds of distractions for an hour? I certainly can't. I give it a try or two and realize that this was yet one more thing I am not good at, so I simply brush that part of Step Eleven under the rug.

Going to meetings regularly not only boosts my mood and sense of meaningful connection, it is where I learn layer upon layer of helpful guidance about how to get the most out of working the steps of recovery, and why I must keep at it, even when I'm completely stuck. And so, simply by showing up, I have a breakthrough in my understanding of prayer and meditation.

Praying is simply having a conversation with your Higher Power. It doesn't have to be anything formal, long, or repetitive, just a casual chat will do. You see, every time you share your thoughts and words with God, the bond grows stronger, and the roots grow deeper into your spirituality.

Meditation became accessible to me once I learned that it's not a matter of clearing your mind as much as becoming aware, especially of the universe around us. I sit comfortably and just listen to the sounds around me and do my best to be present in the moment. As I do this, the noise in my head quiets and I experience life outside of ME!

God just wants a relationship with us, that's all. He wants us to lay the burden of our lives on Him so we can be at peace. When we have peace in our hearts, we can share love more easily, and therefore, we are experiencing God.

Step Eleven…*check!*

Step Twelve: *Having had a spiritual awakening as a result of these steps, we tried to carry this message to addicts, and to practice these principles in all of our affairs.*

"By the time we reach this step, we have experienced a spiritual awakening…" To look at these words "spiritual awakening," one might think this means exactly what it says…an awakening of your spirit. However, a spiritual awakening for me is much more than that. Yes, my spirit, which was once dark and sad, is now awake and bright, but it is beyond that. For me to have this incredible experience, a lot needed to change, both in my behavior and, more importantly, my thought process.

I describe my spiritual awakening in both a literal and figurative sense. When the Bible group prayed for me and I experienced the cravings removal miracle, there was no turning back. At that moment, my spirit opened up to the presence of the Holy Spirit. I was spiritually awakened. The other awakening I experienced was a psychic shift in my thought processes. My normal "go-to" thoughts and behaviors when I was using were destructive and harmful, yet I was unable to recognize or change them. Now, I can identify the negative thoughts and behaviors and NOT follow through on them—by choice.

The real miracle is that I find myself automatically behaving in correct and healthy ways, without me having to even think it through. There's simply no "difficult decision" struggle. That, to me, is a spiritual awakening at its best.

There is a lot to unpack in Step Twelve, but after working through the previous steps with my sponsor and the program support, I am just like other clean and sober women and men I've met in recovery who feel like all they want to do is share this miracle with others.

We have learned to live a life of honesty, openness, and faith. We no longer want to hide in fear or numb our feelings with drugs or alcohol. We have clear and steadfast directions on "how to get through life on life's terms," which is what most of us wanted in the first place.

We may simply feel more joy in our lives, and notice that how we react to a certain stimulus is different. Perhaps we no longer lose our temper so quickly or are quick to cast blame on others. We have a more open and trusting outlook on life and spend more time showing love and compassion toward others than hate and judgment. By the time we reach this step, life looks and feels completely different than when we were in the throes of our addiction.

And because our addictive behaviors commenced as ways to cope with inner wounds, by the time we reach this step, we've experienced so much healing and recovery that for most of us, we now feel better mentally, emotionally, physically, and spiritually than ever before in our lives.

Whatever it is for each person, it is a gift. And once you experience the freedom and love of this gift, you can't help but want to share it with people whose pain we recognize all too well. And that is how we carry the message to others. This is a step about SERVICE. It can look like showing up and sharing at meetings; offering to lead a newcomers' group at a meeting; offering to be a sponsor and guide a fellow addict through step work; or, even writing a book to share one's experience, strength, and hope!

It took me just over a year to complete my twelve steps, only to start over again at the urging of my sponsor. In rehab, we focused only on the first three steps, assuring us we would have solid ground beneath our feet before we started digging deep into our soul. What I share in this book about the steps is an abbreviated version, not to be mistaken or substituted for the complete teachings as found in the Big Books of NA and AA.

Step Twelve…*continues forever!*

10

The Joys of Sponsorship

"I'm not ready!" I protest to Kristen when she suggests that I take on a sponsee; that is, begin meeting with a 12-Step newcomer and, I imagine, being their 24/7 program support person.

"Yes, you are." She then walks me over to the teenager who has raised her hand in the meeting to say that she is in need of a sponsor.

"Hi, Sarah!" Kristen greets her in her usual friendly way, "I'm Kristen and this is Deb. We are so glad you spoke up about needing a sponsor, I know that can be hard to do. It just so happens that Deb is looking to sponsor someone! I'll let you two chat a bit." And off she goes.

"Thank you." Sarah says quietly.

"I am happy to help, but to be truthful, I just celebrated one year of sobriety and you will be my first sponsee...so if you would like someone with more time, I completely understand."

She looks at me and says, "I have no idea what any of this is all about, so I wouldn't know if you were doing a good job or not. I just need someone to help me with this mess."

Understood.

We walk to the parking lot together, making plans for our first step-work meeting, when I notice a woman walking briskly towards us. Sarah is noticeably nervous and uncomfortable at the sight of this woman. When she gets to us, Sarah says flatly, "Hi, Mom, this is Deb. She is going to be my sponsor. Deb, this is my mom, Cynthia."

"Oh, hi!" I respond, and reach out my hand for a friendly shake, which she ignores.

"Exactly how long are these meetings?" she demands, "I have been waiting here for well over fifteen minutes since a group of people left the building. I assume that was when the meeting ended?"

I can feel the tension building between the two and Sarah looks like she is going to cry, so I jump in. "The meeting ended at 7:30, but I wanted to talk to Sarah about being her sponsor and that's why she was late getting out here."

Cynthia looks me up and down before asking, "Sponsor? What is that?"

"A sponsor is someone who has been clean and sober for over a year and helps newcomers through the steps of NA or AA," I reply.

"Precisely how much time will that take?" Cynthia asks. I am getting the sense that she'd had enough of her daughter's poor behavior and wants her fixed as quickly as possible. I don't yet have any idea of what hurt Sarah had caused her mother or what kind of havoc Sarah had possibly wreaked in her family, as addicts usually do. As I had done.

"Well, our first meeting will just be me getting to know her and hearing about how she came to need the program. After that, we will meet weekly and start the steps of NA. For some it takes a year, but for many it can take longer."

"She doesn't drive, so you'll have to come to our house to meet," Cynthia says, sounding quite matter-of-fact.

"Where do you live?" I ask.

"West Hartford. And I will insist on being there when you meet until I know I can trust you and her to be alone in my house." She nearly intimidates me to the point of me leaving right then and there. I could make an excuse about them living too far from me, something, so I didn't have to be around this woman.

I look at Sarah who has been staring at the ground with her hands in her pockets, clearly uncomfortable. More like mortified. My heart breaks for her, I know she is living in an unhealthy environment, with a mother who is very dominating and untrusting. I don't know what has transpired for them to end up in such a negative place, but Sarah is only 17 and clearly needs some support and nurturing. Instead of walking away, I feel a strong inner nudge and hear myself saying, "I totally understand, Cynthia, and I am happy to meet at your house. I'll be there on Tuesday evening at seven, if that works for you."

"Fine," she says as she walks away with Sarah in tow.

Sarah turns around and mouths "I'm sorry" to me. I put my fist to my ear and mouth back "call me."

I immediately call Kristen. "What have I gotten myself into? Sarah's mom is demanding that she be part of our meetings and if they are anything like tonight's encounter, Sarah won't be opening up much."

"Stay focused on Sarah, not her mom." Kristen says. "She is the one who was sitting in that room tonight asking for help. But remember, in order to get through to Sarah, you'll have to start with Cynthia."

That Tuesday I drop Hunter with Kristen and make the half-hour drive to Sarah's house. I knock on the door of their modest bungalow in a cute neighborhood, where it is clear that Cynthia and her neighbors take pride in their homes and property. Their yards are neatly manicured, and the flower gardens are abundant with colors from a variety of different flowers.

Cynthia opens the door before I make it to the front step and extends her arm towards the living room, simply saying, "Come in."

"Hi, thank you." I stammer, being taken back again by her coolness.

"Sarah will be right out. Have a seat and I'll get you some water."

"Okay, thank you." I look at the bottle of water I am holding and wonder why I don't tell her I am all set with a drink. I am already nervous with this being my first meeting with a sponsee, and the frostiness of Cynthia really has me feeling insecure.

The living room is nicely decorated with warm colors, comfy furniture, and on all the walls and table are pictures of Sarah and Cynthia from when Sarah is a baby until her most recent birthday. To my surprise, their home is very welcoming. Looking at the photos, I see no other children, and I sense a lot of love and happiness between the two of them. I also notice there are no pictures of a man or another woman in any of the photos, leading me to believe that Cynthia has raised Sarah on her own.

Cynthia returns, hands me a glass of water, and sits down in a chair. "So, tell me again what you and Sarah will be discussing today?" I sit down on the couch across from her and suddenly feel like I am being interviewed for a job I don't want, but desperately need.

"Well," I begin, "a sponsor is a mentor, if you will, who introduces a newcomer to the fellowship of NA or AA and is responsible for taking them through the twelve steps of the program. I will also make myself available to Sarah if she is struggling or needs advice or direction in her recovery. Today's conversation is about getting to know her and to hear from her what she has been struggling with."

As soon as I finish, Sarah appears in the doorway between the kitchen and living room where we are seated. "Hey! How are you?" I say as I stand and go to hug her.

"Good."

"I was just telling your mom a little about what you and I will be doing together as a sponsor/sponsee. I am eager to get to know you and help you get to work on the steps."

Sarah looks at her mom and Cynthia starts to talk. "I believe that Sarah stole one of my sleeping pills."

I look at Sarah and can tell she wants to disappear. Cynthia is staring at her daughter with disgust and disappointment. I wait patiently for her to continue and get to the part where Sarah did the unspeakable acting out which got her into this mess. There is a long period of silence and I finally realize they are both looking at me, waiting for my response.

"Oh. Okay." I respond and look at Sarah. "Did you?"

"No!" she protests. "I swear I didn't touch them!!"

"Well then, WHERE IS THE PILL SARAH?!"

"I DON'T KNOW MOM! TRY LOOKING IN THE BOTTOM OF YOUR VODKA BOTTLE!"

Oh shit. The gloves are off.

I turn to Cynthia before she can perhaps slap her daughter and say, "Listen, I probably should have been clearer about this before, but I really should only be talking to Sarah about her situation. May I have some time with her alone?"

"Absolutely not."

"MOM!!" Sarah shouts. "You wanted me to find someone to talk to and now you won't leave us alone! YOU ARE FUCKING CRAZY!"

And with that, Sarah goes stomping down the hallway where she slams her bedroom door so hard that a picture of her and her mom that was secured on the wall comes crashing down to the floor.

I reach over to pick up the picture and check the damage. Luckily, the photo is in perfect shape—but the two people inside the frame are horribly broken.

I look to Cynthia who is on the couch with her head in her hands. I feel uncomfortable being part of such an emotionally charged argument between two people I have just met, but something is urging me to stay and help if I can.

I know I will be taking a risk that Cynthia will accost me with her unpleasantness again if I don't leave, but I figure it may be worth the risk. "I am sorry things are so tough between you two right now," I say, and gently sit next to Cynthia.

She is still for a moment before she takes a deep breath, stands up, and without a shred of emotion, says, "You can go now."

I want so badly to grab my purse and run from that house, but instead I say, "I would rather stay and talk a while. Maybe I can be helpful if I get a little more information about what is happening with Sarah. It's clear you both are very close and there is a lot of love between you two, but it's also apparent there is mistrust and pain. If she really does have a drug problem, I think I can be of help to both of you."

I have no idea where this is all coming from. Who am I to say I may be able to help? I am barely holding on myself, but I guess this is all part of working my Step Twelve: "Having had a spiritual awakening as a result of these steps, we try to carry this message to addicts, and to practice these principles in all our affairs."

Cynthia stands up and walks into the kitchen without saying a word. I take that as my cue to go and start gathering my things. Before I know it, she is back in the living room with a glass of wine in one hand and a cigarette in the other.

"Fine, let's talk," she says flatly.

We sit outside on the back patio for over an hour. The first few minutes are quiet, but once the wine kicks in, an entirely new Cynthia emerges.

Glass #1: Cynthia shares that Sarah's dad was never in the picture. It was a brief relationship when Cynthia is 18 that ends the moment she tells him the news of the pregnancy. Cynthia's family all but disowns her, so she is on her own. I learn that she comes from a mixed-race family where her father is white and her mother is Black. Cynthia suffers at the hands of cruel children when she is young and a racist society as she gets older.

Glass #2: When her parents kick her out, she calls a friend who she is working with at a local bakery and sleeps on her couch for the next three months until she finds a room to rent. She is constantly tired and suffers terrible nausea during the pregnancy, but always shows up for work at 5 a.m. and works a 10–12-hour day. Cynthia sounds proud as she shares that she's always had a strong work ethic and, "I still do, to this very day."

Glass #3: The slurring starts as she continues. She manages to put herself through graduate school and now has a prestigious position as an executive at a large insurance company in Hartford.

She is highly educated and successful, yet feels that she will never be seen as anything more than a Black, single mother. "Society doesn't care how smart you are or how hard you work. I keep telling Sarah that she MUST BE HER BEST AT ALL TIMES!"

Glass #4: Slurring is much worse, and she has lit the wrong end of her cigarette...again.

"Sarah is doing drugs!" she exclaims. "I just know it!"

I finally get a chance to chime in. "What makes you say that? Have you found any or caught her doing drugs?"

"A sllleeeepiinngg pill is misssinnngg!" she slurs at me. "Didn't you heeeaaarrrr that earlier??"

It is becoming clear to me that there will be no productive conversation at this point. Now I don't know what to do. I can't just leave this drunk, babbling woman to her own devices, but I really, really, want to leave.

I excuse myself to go to the bathroom, go inside and gently knock on Sarah's door. There is no answer and I panic, thinking that she has left the house. I knock again, louder. In desperation, I open the door. To my relief she is there with her headphones on, listening to some sort of loud music. She doesn't realize I am there and I hate to touch her and risk scaring her to death, so I grab one of her small stuffed animals and toss it at her foot. This does the trick. She takes off her headphones and is clearly surprised to see me. "I thought you left a while ago."

"No, I have been out back with your mom, hoping to have a chat, but things have gone a bit sideways."

She rolls her eyes. "Let me guess, she's drunk."

"Yes, she is. I don't know what to do."

Sarah makes her way past me. I follow her outside, where we find her mom happily singing and twirling around all by herself. I hold my breath, waiting for another fight to ensue, but what I witness is incredibly sad and beautiful at the same time.

Sarah approaches her mom and gently coaxes her. "Come on Mom, let's go take a nap."

Cynthia looks at Sarah with such love and adoration and takes her daughter's face in her hands. "You are my everything."

"I know, Mom. I love you and we are going to take a nap now."

"Will you nap with me?" she asks in a childlike way.

"Yes Mom, I will."

I realize that this ritual happens on far more than one occasion and that it is not Sarah who needs help, it is her mom.

I follow, not saying anything, as Sarah leads her mom to her bedroom. She helps her take off her shoes and tucks her in. "I'll be right back, Mom."

She walks me to the front door and apologizes. "Please do not apologize," I say. "There is no need to. How long has this been going on?"

"For a while now, but it has gotten worse in the past six months. I think it's because I am talking about going away to college next year. I am all she has, and she can't handle the thought of me going away."

"What is all this about the missing pill and bringing you to an NA meeting?" I ask.

"She swears I took it, but I didn't. You can clearly see she is in no shape to keep track of her pills."

We can hear Cynthia calling for her, so we say our goodbyes and I ask her to please keep in touch. I tell her that I would be happy to get her mom connected in AA if and when she is ready.

I call Kristen on my way home and tell her the entire crazy story.

"Wow!" she replies, "that is God working in their lives."

"Really?" I challenge, "I don't see God anywhere in that mess."

"It is pretty clear that Cynthia has a drinking problem," she says, "and she is deflecting and projecting her issues onto Sarah." I agree.

"The missing pill leads to Cynthia forcing Sarah to go to an NA meeting, which leads to meeting you," Kristen says. "That is what ultimately exposes what is really going on. Now we can focus our energy on Cynthia, who is the one suffering with a disease. God knows this would be the only way to uncover the truth."

"Now what?" I ask.

"Keep in close touch with Sarah and see how the events of today unfold with Cynthia. When the door opens, we will be ready for her."

"What if the door remains tightly closed and dead-bolted?" I ask.

"Then we keep on praying until she is ready."

Sarah and I keep close contact for several months after that day at her house. I help her as much as I can by educating her on the disease of addiction and alcoholism. The more I teach her, the more I also learn. It is clear by now that Sarah does not have a problem with drugs or alcohol so there is no reason for her to attend NA meetings or have a sponsor in that fellowship, but she desperately needs a friend or two who can relate to what she is and has been going through. She attends some Al-Anon meetings but doesn't feel she can relate to the members seeing as they are much older and mostly speak about their spouses or children who suffer from the disease. Where she does find support and friendships is through Alateen meetings. Alateen is a fellowship of young people who are often the children of an addict and/or alcoholic. Alateen aligns with Sarah's needs, and she is able to forge a path through the chaos of her homelife. She learns to build a healthy boundary with her mother and not let Cynthia's behaviors and actions take away her peace. It is a daily battle to keep those lines clear and protect herself from her mother's frequent assaults, but she does her best with the tools she is given in the fellowship.

Her mother refuses to acknowledge her own addictive, destructive behavior and continues to give Sarah a hard time until the day she leaves for college…in California. It is the farthest she can go to get away from the drama and dysfunction of her home.

Before she leaves, Sarah strategically places around their home multiple AA pamphlets which list the dates and times of meetings.

By Christmas, her mom has been fired for being drunk at work and declines to take a leave to go to rehab. Sarah has been thriving at school and can't bear the thought of flying across the country to spend a miserable Christmas with her alcoholic mother. When she breaks the news that she isn't coming home and why, Cynthia finally breaks. For her, this is unbearable; this is hitting bottom.

She looks frantically for one of those AA pamphlets and prays out loud to God, hoping she hasn't thrown all of them away. She finally finds one at the very bottom of the linen closet where Sarah knew that Cynthia loved to hide her bottles.

On December 20, 2005, Cynthia arrives at the 7:30 p.m. women's meeting of AA, raises her hand, and asks for help. Cynthia will celebrate 18 years of sobriety this December. She has helped countless women in recovery as an inspiration and as a sponsor herself. Cynthia shares her story of brokenness, healing, and how she finally finds peace and joy in her life. Her daughter Sarah is a successful therapist specializing in Adult Children of Alcoholics.

God certainly does have a plan. He always does.

CHAPTER
11

My Worlds Collide

"Don't give up until the miracle happens." When it comes to sponsoring women, I am ready to throw in the towel, despite this oft-repeated NA slogan.

Sarah, the teenager I shared about in the previous chapter, is in an unusual situation, which ultimately has a happy ending. My next four sponsees are a different story. One of them attempts to take her own life (thankfully, she is unsuccessful). Another relapses within minutes of completing the first step; the third waits until we have spent hours together, painstakingly doing her fourth step before going off the rails. And the fourth woman...she is doing great until, well, you'll read about that soon.

"Sponsorship is not for me," I declare to my sponsor Kristen.

"You're right, it's not for you. It's for them."

I shake my head at her, not wanting to hear what she is saying. "No one listens to me anyway!" I whine. "It's frustrating spending so much time with someone, caring about them and their wellbeing and then, just when you think you're making progress—poof! They are out the door!"

"I know, it's difficult. You become so attached."

"So, you understand if I don't take on any more sponsees for a while?" I ask, holding my crossed fingers up.

She laughs and says, "No. Your Step Twelve work is important to you. And, it's your responsibility to help others. Think about when you first came into the rooms and imagine if no one offered to help you. We are all mentally, emotionally, and spiritually sick when we first come into recovery, some more than others. You'll learn to decipher who is ready and who isn't, and you'll adjust your time and energy based on how willing they are to receive your help."

That piece of advice still holds true. When I am asked to sponsor someone, I always tell them, "I'll give you the same time and energy that you give to me. If you give me 100%, I'll do the same, but the minute I feel you are wasting my time, I'm out. There are lots of women who really want to get clean and sober who I can give my time to."

I have stopped blaming myself for their decisions. I have come to learn that I have to stay focused on my recovery and not base my feelings of success or failure on other people's choices.

"Look," Kristen says, "you have five years under your belt now, so you obviously know how to remain clean and sober. It's imperative for your own recovery that you share your knowledge with others. That's why we say you must give it away in order to keep it. So, stop complaining and start praying for a sponsee to come into your life."

I meet Gail at a meeting and instantly love her energy. She is easygoing, pleasant, and eager to get sober. It is effortless to strike up a conversation, since we have a lot in common. She is a single mother, working to make ends meet, and wants desperately to stop drinking and drugging her way through life. She has been in the fellowship of NA previously, years before, and managed to stay clean and sober for ten years before picking up a drink to help her through a very painful breakup with a man she had believed she would marry.

It should not have been a surprise that it doesn't work out—for one thing, he is her boss, and for another, he is married. When he breaks the news that he has come clean to his wife and they have decided to work on their marriage, she is devastated. There are years of promises made to her that they would one day be together, and that she just needed to be patient. As if the breakup isn't painful enough, he also informs her that she will no longer be employed at their place of business.

She cries, screams, and begs him not to do this, but her pleading falls on deaf ears. When her emotional temper tantrum doesn't get his attention and save her job (and her heart), her rage kicks in and she threatens to sue him. Then the gloves are off and for the next year and a half they battle it out in court—Gail, asking for enough money to set him back years (out of spite, of course), the ex, not wanting to give her a dime.

In the end, they settle on an amount that would barely cover her attorney fees. She is defeated, deflated, and spiritually bankrupt.

While her children wait for her to come home after court, she drives to the closest bar and orders a shot of whiskey and a beer. And just like that, she is right back where she starts. Ten years of sobriety, meetings, step work, sponsorship, service work, healthy relationships with her kids, family, and friends. All of it...out the window.

She would like to tell me that it is just a "slip," a one-night bender to numb her pain, but addiction doesn't work like that. Our disease is a progressive one that will fight like hell to keep you sick, and once you fight it off, it waits patiently for you to visit again. Quiet and sly, it lurks in the mind's darkest corner, just waiting for the smallest crack to open. It whispers seductive, convincing justifications. It flows out of hiding and into all of our being. We feel it in every cell of our body, that unbearable itch that demands to be scratched. And even though we know that the more we scratch, the more persistent the itch becomes, we do it anyway, because we long for the few moments of relief it allows.

Gail's disease kicks into gear and hijacks her hard-won sobriety. Within three short months, she loses her children, is evicted from her apartment, and lives in her car. She makes money to support her drug habit by driving dealers around to their customers. Often, in exchange for her service, she gets a big rock of crack cocaine. If she is lucky, she doesn't get robbed or beat up, but most of the time she isn't.

A dealer she is helping punches her in the face, shattering her nose and left cheekbone. Then he drags her out of the driver's seat, throws her on the ground, kicks her in the ribs, and backs the car over her leg.

She still does not recall how she gets to the hospital, but it is there that she spends over two months recuperating from the assault and multiple surgeries. That is how Gail hits bottom.

During those multiple weeks, she has only one visitor—just one person who shows up every week to sit by her bedside and pray for her while she sleeps. One person who brings her magazines, books, and homemade banana bread. One person who makes her feel worthy of love and compassion—her sponsor.

Gail's sponsor Christine has never given up on her, has always held Gail in her heart and prayed for her, even after Gail makes it clear she is no longer participating in recovery. She has fallen off the wagon and refuses to accept a hand up and back into sobriety. Christine frequently calls the local hospitals and county jails to track Gail down, so she isn't surprised to get an anonymous call one night from the hospital: "Someone you know is here."

When Gail wakes up from surgery and sees Christine, she thinks she is hallucinating. *Why in the world is she here?* she asks herself. She is still drowsy from the anesthesia and pain meds when she wakes up later and again, thinks she sees Christine sitting by her bedside. She drifts back to sleep and for the next three days is in and out of a foggy, drugged state. On day four, they start cutting back on the Dilaudid®, and Gail's head becomes clearer. She looks around the room and sees no sign of any visitors. She is convinced that her visions of Christine are not real.

Later that day, Gail is flabbergasted when Christine walks in with a big bouquet of flowers, wearing the most warm and beautiful smile. "Well, you finally decide to wake up!"

Christine says as she sets the flowers on the nightstand. She gently hugs Gail and whispers, "I've got you. You're not alone." Gail melts into Christine's arms and sobs.

Kristen and I are sobbing ourselves after hearing this incredible story. There is nothing more powerful than an addict's story of hitting bottom and then finding such kindness and compassion there.

"I have been clean and sober since then," Gail says. "I haven't gotten my kids back, but I am working on it. I am renting a room in a house and working part-time. Christine and I are working the steps again and I just finished Step Ten. Last week she calls to tell me that her husband is in poor health, and they will be moving into an assisted living facility near their daughter in Boston. She suggests I get a new sponsor."

Once again, I get the look from Kristen and then the words come. "I'm sorry to hear about Christine," Kristen says to her. "You two have a really special connection which will be hard to replace. However, Deb was just saying how she wishes she had another sponsee to work with."

Gail's eyes light up. "Really? Oh, that would be amazing. I was dreading having to ask the group for fear of someone I didn't like coming forward to volunteer."

"I would be honored to sponsor you," I say, and give her the ol' "I'm in 100% as long as you are…" speech.

So, we start meeting every week, working on the steps and getting to know each other. Gail no longer has a car, so we spend a lot of time driving to meetings and going to social events together. She is gentle, kind, and fierce all at the same time. Her sense of humor is epic and when Kristen, Gail, and I get together, we have side-splitting laughter for hours. I realize that these joy-filled times would never have happened if I'd tried to stay sober by myself. Having my sponsor on one side and my sponsee on the other keeps me solidly on Recovery Road.

I am so proud of Gail when she celebrates her second year in recovery. She has done the steps twice, at her request, and has started to sponsor two women. She has an apartment where her kids are allowed to visit twice a week. She has an entry-level job that is far beneath her earning capabilities, but it allows her to make ends meet. She has been working really hard on herself and is making incredible strides. My heart is filled with joy for her.

And then, my worlds collide.

Gail is at my apartment one night when my ex-husband stops by to see Hunter. At that time, Trevor is working as an outside sales rep for a manufacturing company. He has a home office in his condo, but spends most of his time driving through his territory, Connecticut to Maine. On this day, he has just come back from driving most of the day and calls to ask if he can pick up Hunter to go out for a bite. I tell him I already have dinner cooking, and ask if he would like to join us instead of going out.

"My ex-husband is coming for dinner," I tell Gail. "You and I will be done meeting before he gets here, but you're welcome to stay for dinner and a show, as I'm fairly certain he is high."

"Sure!" Gail says. "I would love some food and entertainment! That's so great that you invite him to dinner. I don't know anyone who would do that."

I tell her that I am not doing this out of the kindness of my heart, but rather to keep Hunter from getting in the car with someone who most likely is under the influence of some substance. I have learned a long time ago not to tell him the truth about why I don't want him driving Hunter anywhere, and have become practiced at having alternate options to suggest. This is one of those times.

"Is he going to care that I am here?"

"Not at all, and to protect your anonymity, I won't share with him that I am your sponsor or that you are in the program, so if he asks where we met, just say through mutual friends."

"Oh, I don't care about that. I am very open about my sobriety."

"Okay, whatever you are comfortable with."

Trevor arrives around 6:30 p.m. reeking of marijuana, and I thank God for not letting Hunter get in a car with him.

I introduce him to Gail and tell him to feel free to go see Hunter in his room, or he can call him downstairs, whatever he wants.

As he walks towards the stairs, I catch a glimpse of Gail following him with her eyes. *Oh shit.*

Trevor's a very good-looking man, like movie star good looks. Tall and tan (no matter what season it is), with thick hair and deep brown eyes. He knows how to dress and always takes pride in his wardrobe. In addition to his good looks, he has a way of making a woman feel like she is the most interesting and beautiful person he has ever met. This is a dangerous combination and has caused many women to fall hard for him, only to be left with a crushing heartache and their self-esteem in the toilet. No woman is safe around him. If he wants you, he is going to get you. Period.

I watch the two of them closely at dinner and am happy to see that Trevor's attention is mostly on Hunter and not Gail. He wants to hear about every minute of Hunter's week and also to tell us tales of his trip to Maine. I think to myself, *Wow, I can't believe he isn't focusing all his attention on Gail.* Our dinner turns out to be stress-free and dare I say...enjoyable?

Trevor gets Hunter ready for bed after dinner, while Gail and I clean up in the kitchen. "He seems nice," she says quite casually. "He certainly loves Hunter."

"Yes," I respond. "Despite all the shit we have been through, I can honestly say that he loves Hunter and has always done right by him. I mean, don't get me wrong, he has made some stupid and reckless decisions at times, but I can't take away the fact that Hunter is his whole heart."

We sit to have a cup of coffee when Trevor walks downstairs and out the front door. A few minutes later, he is back, along with the strong smell of weed.

"Couldn't you wait until you leave to smoke?" I say. "Have some respect for our recovery."

"Shit, I didn't think of that. I'm sorry. I'll go wash my hands."

"Like that will help," I say to Gail with a roll of my eyes.

He sits down with us and starts complaining about how stressed he is with work. "I can't seem to keep my expense reports up to date and the lady at work is giving me shit about it. I have more important things to do than keep track of every single receipt I get for a Diet Coke!" he vents.

"Just throw them in an envelope and every night, plug the info into your computer." I say. "Then you won't get behind and overwhelmed."

"It's not as easy as you make it sound. I have hundreds of receipts after a week-long trip.

What I need is to hire someone who can take care of all that admin shit. I need to stay focused on selling!"

"I can help," Gail says. "I am super organized and could use some extra money."

Trevor looks at her and smiles. "That would be great! Thanks!"

What a terrible idea. I immediately know this is bad news. Gail is single and vulnerable, and easy prey for Trevor.

"Maybe we need to talk this through, Gail. I don't think it's a good idea for you to take on too much. Your recovery needs all of your focus right now."

"Oh, okay," she says.

Trevor shoots me a nasty look and I know I am going to get an ear full from him, but I don't care. I will take the bullet for her.

I walk him out to his car and before he can start in on me, I blast him. "There is no way you are hiring her! She is way too vulnerable with her recovery and I don't trust you for a second!"

"Deb, I would NEVER do anything to put her or anyone else in recovery in jeopardy. I have far too much respect for you and everyone trying to get clean. I really need some help. Even if it's just to get me caught up on the past month, that would be a huge help. It would literally take her a few hours and then I would be able to manage on my own."

"No. Find someone else."

"Jesus, Deb, she's an adult. You don't get a say in what she can and can't do!"

"When it comes to you, yes, I do. Don't tell me you have respect for people in recovery! You couldn't be here for two hours without being so high we could smell the weed before you even got out of the car! You knew there would be sober people here AND your 8-year-old son!" I can feel him preparing his rebuttal, so I walk back inside before all hell breaks loose. I hear him drive off and am happy that the argument doesn't escalate. I am pretty amazed that he doesn't retaliate in any way and lets me have the last word for once in our lives.

I return to the kitchen to find Gail getting ready to head out. "Please, before you go, I want to explain why I don't think it's a good idea to work for him."

She sits back down and focuses in on what I am about to say. "Trevor may seem like the nicest guy in the world, and it may look like he has his shit together, but he is very sick in his disease. He struggles with addiction for several years now and refuses to even acknowledge that he has a problem. I won't get into the nitty gritty of it all, but I feel very strongly that if you are alone with him, he will take advantage of you and I don't want to see you get hurt or put your recovery at risk."

"I understand and I appreciate you looking after me. You're right, it wouldn't be a good idea."

I am relieved to hear that she is going to let it go. We schedule our time to meet the following week, hug each other goodbye, and off she goes.

Two days later I find her on Trevor's couch, stoned.

They aren't expecting me, obviously. I have only gone over after receiving a call from a friend who lives in the same condo complex as Trevor. She causally mentions seeing Gail drive by while on a walk. "I see her turn onto the road Trevor lives on. What a coincidence that she knows someone on that road," my friend says.

I don't knock. The door is always unlocked. The condo is cluttered, dirty, and smells of skunk weed. They are both on the couch, high, watching TV. Gail sinks down into the couch when she sees me. Trevor, wearing only boxer shorts, jumps up.

"Jesus! What the hell are you doing here?"

He follows me to the kitchen where I calmly say, "There were a lot of things that you did to me that were disgusting and disgraceful during the last years of our marriage, but nothing that you've done to me is as despicable as what you have done to her." My calmness starts to dissipate as I continue.

"You are taking away two years of her hard work in recovery. TWO YEARS! Do you have any idea what you have done?! She is inches away from getting her life back! Inches away from getting her KIDS back! You and your selfishness have quite possibly sent her back to the streets…"

Before I can continue, he interrupts and simply says, "She does it to herself."

I feel rage pour through my veins like I have never felt before. Before I know it, I pounce on him, pounding my fists into his chest and screaming, "You are such a piece of shit! I HATE YOU!"

Trevor is 6'3" and I am a full foot shorter than him, so my assault on him is in vain, but I can't deny it feels good to get years of frustration and upset out of my system.

While this scene unfolds in the kitchen, Gail is hiding in the bathroom. Knowing that nothing I say or do will make Trevor take responsibility, I turn my focus on Gail.

I knock on the bathroom door. "Can I come in?"

No answer. I try the door…locked.

"Gail, please let me in," I plead, "I just want to know that you are okay."

She opens the door and drops to the floor, sitting with her head in her hands. I sit down next to her and just let her cry.

"I am so ashamed."

"Don't be. Feeling shameful will only make things worse. You made a mistake, that's all. You aren't the first to relapse and sadly, won't be the last. You have a choice to make, though."

"Do you want to continue on this path, or resume your journey in recovery?" I ask.

"I am so close to getting my kids back and I blew it!" she says, still sobbing.

"Look, you are clean for two years and have a two-day relapse. If you come with me now, we can grab a coffee and hit a meeting. It is never too late to start over."

We sit in silence for a while, and when there are no more tears to cry, she stands up, looks at me and says, "Let's go."

When we walk out of the condo, Trevor is nowhere to be seen.

The road to recovery not only has many potholes and blind corners, it has many forks—the addict must choose clean living, or not, again and again. I am very relieved that my sponsee, in that moment, chooses living free over staying sick. That pretty much sums up the role of a sponsor: shine a light on the best path to take at every fork in the addict's rough road, while knowing that it's the sponsee's choice to make.

The following year, Gail moves into her own apartment and is granted shared custody of her children. She has been promoted at work to a management position and she mentors women in crisis.

I don't quit on her, and she doesn't quit on herself, and that is the miracle of sponsorship.

CHAPTER

12

My Sponsor and Me Against the World

There is an art to finding the right sponsor. You have to know what type of personality inspires you to stay clean and sober. For example, there are sponsors who are very structured, have clear "rules," such as requiring a phone call every morning and expecting a synopsis of what you are doing that day. They will, no doubt, add to your day's plan by assigning some NA reading or service work. These (what I call) sergeant sponsors are not interested in forging a friendship with you. They do not chit-chat about the weather, but they listen intently to you (both what you say and don't say) and hold you accountable. They are there for one purpose only, to show you how to stay clean. This type of sponsor is not for me. But for some, without this disciplined approach, they would not be successful in recovery.

On the other end of the sponsoring style continuum, there are angels who float along with you but don't insert themselves into your reality. They can seem so laid back that it leaves you to wonder if they remember you are their sponsee. Reaching out for help meets with, "Well, honey, just pray about it. You'll figure it out." Even when the angel sponsor is called in desperation because you just discovered a bag of cocaine in an old duffle bag, you won't get "orders" about what to do, but rather, "Now, pray about it. You'll figure it out." Some women I know thrive with an angel sponsor because they can figure it out and prefer not to be told what to do. For me, when I am newly sober, I am not able to figure out how to empty a dishwasher, let alone get myself out of a tempting situation, so this type of sponsor is not for me.

The other type of sponsor is the one I am lucky enough to be tethered to. My sponsor and I quickly become allies, united in our shared commitment to sobriety and well-being. With Kristen as my ally sponsor, I feel that there is hope. She has just enough toughness to teach me boundaries and show me when I am heading in the wrong direction, and enough aloofness to give me space to figure shit out on my own. But the best part of having Kristen as my sponsor is that she becomes my best friend. This is unusual in a sponsor/sponsee relationship. Some become friends and often good friends, but to have the closeness that we have is uncommon.

I rent one of the tiny mill houses among a cluster of these 100-year-old structures that were originally built to house the workers of a nearby mill. It seems as though people back then were quite miniature, as I am 5'3" and have to duck my head while going up the stairs to what once was an attic but now serves as bedrooms. In addition to the tiny frame of the house, I also find that our neighborhood has a "unique" cast of characters.

On more than one occasion I find my elderly next-door neighbor Ray sitting on my couch. He has dementia and often escapes from his house and comes to mine. Hunter lets him in and they watch TV together until his family notices he is gone and comes over to fetch him. Overall, he is harmless, but on one occasion Hunter comes upstairs and informs me that Ray is downstairs telling "dirty jokes" to a room full of Hunter's friends. I rush down the stairs, smack my head on the low ceiling, and fall ass-over-teakettle down the rest of the steep, narrow stairs. By the time I am downstairs and on my feet again, Ray has been retrieved and gone home.

It is times like these that I wish I had a husband to step in and help. I try to assess the damage by questioning the boys, but they are not about to share what they've heard with me. I know these boys have both a mom and a dad at home, so I tell them to talk to their dads, especially if they have any questions about what Mr. Ray was talking about. I then call to let the parents know what has transpired. Most of the parents are understanding and just laugh it off, but one mother decides to chastise me for "letting an old pervert just walk into a house full of children." My apology falls on deaf ears. Within minutes, her husband is at my door to collect his son. This is just one example of multiple times that I wish it isn't just me. I am certain my make-believe husband would have handled the situation much better than I have.

Now, Kristen…she has it made, and I envy her. She is married to her high school sweetheart, has two adorable children, a beautiful home, and a husband who is there and active in the kids' life. All decisions are made together, and idyllic family trips are taken frequently. I long for that "white picket fence" home life. Not to mention the financial freedom that comes with a responsible husband and dual incomes!

I work full-time but can never manage to make ends meet. My credit card debt piles up. I am constantly late signing Hunter up for sports or extracurricular activities. It is all I can do to make sure he has lunch money every day (I have given up on making him lunch). I often forget and some nice lunch lady gives him money. I feel the weight of the world on my shoulders every day. I am working now, but there is never any extra money to spare. Child support is so sporadic I can't count on that, and I refuse to ask for help from my parents since I still owe a financial amends to them. In order to pay them back for my legal fees, I sell all my good jewelry and am out of anything of value to hawk. My financial fears wake me many nights and the worry suffocates me.

The first year of my recovery I spend one day a week at Kristen's doing Step work and usually another time or two at her house for dinner or just hanging out while the kids romp around. She and her husband Kyle pretty much adopt Hunter and me, including us in many family outings.

Around the second year is when I start sensing the tension between them rising up to a notable level. She often voices her frustration about him with me and I support her as best as I can, but I honestly cannot understand why she is so unhappy with a life I would give anything for. Sure, I notice his impatience with her and his occasional snarky comment toward her, but isn't that normal in a marriage?

I remember her asking me what she should do as she contemplates divorce and my response is, "If you and the kids aren't in physical danger, I would stick it out. You've got a great set-up!"

My desire to have what she has clouds my ability to see how truly unhappy she is. It isn't a matter of what she has, it is how empty she feels inside. She and her husband marry after learning she is pregnant. That's always tricky, even though they have known each other for years. There is a love between them for certain, however, she often wonders…

I should mention that, as addicts, we tend to be ridiculously co-dependent and extreme people pleasers. Often, the object of our desire relishes the attention and neediness we lavish upon them, meeting the needs of both parties involved. Kristen and her husband fit this mold perfectly. She longs to meet his every need and he gladly accepts her offerings, but rarely returns the favor, leaving Kristen feeling emotionally empty.

As she grows in her sobriety, she works diligently on balancing her needs with those of others, ultimately learning to make her own needs a priority. This is healthy progress for Kristen, but quite an unwelcome change for her husband. When a relationship is built on a certain dynamic and one person starts to alter the unspoken "contract" which has been in place for years, the foundation crumbles. Confusion ensues, feelings are hurt, fights erupt, and in the case of Kristen and her husband, the contract dissolves. The following year they are officially divorced.

Vowing to never put another man's needs in front of her own, Kristen moves out and begins to transform herself and her life. She buys a house of her own, gets a job, and even dips her toe into the dating scene. Fortunately, she and her children's father remain on good terms, sharing custody and maintaining mutual respect. No hard feelings or resentments, no harsh words or petty spats. It is so unlike my divorce that I truly wonder if they really should have split up.

And then comes Kathy. "Kyle has a girlfriend!" Kristen is frantic.

"No way! Who?" I can't help but be startled. For one, Kyle is shy and uncomfortable around anyone who is not in his small inner circle, and secondly, he has never been with anyone except for Kristen. The thought of him being with anyone else never crosses my mind. I know that Kristen is open to exploring other relationships, but Kyle? No way.

"Someone named Kathy. They have been dating for a few weeks. Jessica just told me about her!"

I try to calm her down, while I struggle to understand why she is coming undone.

"Listen, I am sure this is not a long-term thing. Let's face it, Kyle isn't the easiest person to be with. I'm sure she will figure that out soon enough. More importantly, how come you're so upset?"

"I just never thought he would find someone else! I haven't met anyone and now I feel like he is moving on and I am going to be alone forever!"

Fear. Nothing takes us down faster than fear of the unknown, especially when it comes to matters of the heart. As Kyle and Kathy's relationship grows, Kristen's fear becomes overwhelming. The news of Kathy and her daughter moving in with Kyle sends her over the edge.

Kristen is convinced that they will be living as a happy family and will want to take full custody of her children. She worries that because her new house is outside of the kids' school district, she may lose custody. So, in a rash decision, she quickly sells her beloved little home and ends up in a small apartment in a less desirable area, close to Kyle and Kathy. Meanwhile, Kyle has no intention of fighting her for custody, and within six months of Kathy moving in, she moves out. All that Kristen fears never comes to fruition. The time, energy, emotions, and money that she expends are all in vain—the perfect example of "False Evidence Appearing Real."

Fear drives us to make decisions that are rarely in our best interest. For me, my fear of financial insecurity drives me to a decision that ends up causing people I care about great pain.

"I'm thinking about moving in with Matthew," I blurt out one day when Kristen and I are having coffee at my place.

"Oh my God! That's awesome! Matthew is a great guy!" she says, excited for me. Her response gives me some confidence about a decision I have been struggling with. Matthew and I have been dating for several months. He is a solid, kind, dependable man who adores Hunter, and the feeling is mutual. Moving in together seems like the logical next step in our relationship, but I am feeling unsettled about it. Deep down I know my motives may not have been pure.

"What if it doesn't work out?" I ask.

"What if it does?" she retorts.

"What will I do if he turns on me once he knows we have nowhere to go?"

"What if he doesn't turn on you, and you have a wonderful life together? Turn the script around." She continues, "Look for all the amazing things that could happen if you give it a try. He isn't asking you to marry him, just cohabitate. Think of how much money you'll save not having to pay rent. You'll finally be able to get out of the red."

I would be lying if I say I don't think about all the practical ways this will make my life easier. I can have some financial freedom and Hunter will have a wonderful male role model in his life. There are far more pros than cons in this scenario, so I pack up our belongings and take a leap of faith. What I fail to bring to the surface is the truth of my feelings. Matthew has become someone I can trust and lean on, but here's the thing—the more I grow in my recovery, the less I need a man or anyone else to make me feel secure. With the help of my Higher Power, I am filling that need all on my own, by learning that I have worth and value.

A year later, Kristen pulls up in a borrowed truck to help me load all of my things, while Matthew sits in his back yard, alone with a bottle of Captain Morgan's.

There has been no drama, trauma, or abuse. No terrible fight where we say hurtful things that will sting for years to come. He treats me with love and respect and gives his heart and soul to my son, which I will always be grateful to him for. I have everything I've wanted for myself and Hunter, but there is something missing and

I can never put my finger on it. I just know instinctively that this is not meant to be, and I finally understand why Kristen leaves the comfort of her home and husband.

Sometimes you simply outgrow a relationship, especially when you are spending a great deal of time on improving yourself. Personal growth means change, and many times a partner resists that, preferring the person they were initially attracted to. As one program buddy shares, her husband hinders, not helps, her recovery. "I wish you'd never stopped drinking. You're no fun anymore!" But as an addict, we must continue to strive to move forward and improve ourselves. If we don't, then we risk the chance of either becoming stagnant in our recovery or moving backwards, which will only lead to relapse.

We must uncover the parts of us that keep us sick in our disease and learn to identify and change those thoughts and behaviors. In Kristen's case, she is a people-pleaser at an early age, making sure everyone around her is happy and that their needs are met. The positive reinforcement of this behavior makes her feel worthy of being loved. However, the constant attention to others' needs weighs her down and drains her. She turns to drugs, alcohol, and men to fill the emptiness. As she grows older, she carries that character trait into her relationship with Kyle.

The only way to end her destructive behavior is to identify why she feels so empty and then begin to place healthy boundaries around herself. She needs to "re-train" people who expect more from her than she is able or willing to offer, and one of those people is Kyle. In the end, the husband/wife relationship no longer suits either of them.

Now, Kristen and I are both sober, single moms, learning together how to navigate through life, and I thank God for her friendship every day. Hunter and I stay with her until I find a small condo to purchase, using money I have been able to save during the previous year as a down payment. The condo happens to be in Avon, the same town I grew up in. My life is coming full circle. Kristen helps me paint and decorate while we celebrate each other's triumphs over life's challenging situations.

Hunter and I move and I immediately enroll him in summer Little League, where he can make friends that are going to be in his new school. It works out for both of us, as I am able to meet other parents and make friends myself. We settle in nicely and I have the added benefit of reconnecting with some old high school friends who have also moved back to Avon to raise their children.

At one of the ball practices, I am approached by a beautiful woman with long dark hair and blue eyes. I would never have recognized her if she didn't introduce herself and remind me that we went to high school together. Jen has one son, Sam, who is Hunter's age. Jen is also divorced and single, and her son and Hunter become fast friends, as do Jen and I. Between my 12-Step friends and the women in our area, I am surrounded by a small group of women who become my inner circle for years to come, and boy, do I need them.

Kristen and I stay close, of course, but I soon find myself moved down on her priority list. And it is all my fault. What happens is that I introduce her to another parent while we are cheering on Hunter at a game. Pete is divorced and has shared custody of his three kids, with one on the same team as Hunter. Kristen and Pete hit it off immediately and their relationship is in full throttle before the end of the baseball season. I am happy to see she has found someone to share her life with who seems to be kind to her and her kids. Like most new relationships, they spend as much time together as possible, which is an adjustment for me, but worth it to see her so happy. Or so I think.

13

The Walls Come Crumbling Down

January 8, 2013. Hunter is 13 years old. I am just over 9 years clean and sober.

We are at the walk-in clinic at 7:15 p.m. on a Tuesday evening. Hunter has been complaining for over a month about pain in his leg near his left knee. He is growing like a weed, so I contribute it to growing pains, and for over two months I've disregarded his complaints. Now he is refusing to go to basketball practice (which he loves) because of the pain.

"Fine," I say, aggravated. "Just to make you feel better, let's go get an x-ray."

I am annoyed for multiple reasons. First, my son was always accident-prone, and I felt he would often make a mountain out of a molehill when it came to a scrape or bump (in hindsight, I believe he has some internal instinct to pay close attention to his body and not ignore an injury of any kind). Secondly, I often used the 90 minutes during his practice to run errands and we desperately needed some groceries. Lastly, I knew the visit would cost me money that I did not have.

We wait in the exam room, goofing around and taking pictures of Hunter in his paper gown. This becomes the last memory I have before life turned upside down and sideways. In a moment, everything changed, twisting and turning us into a flurry of fear and anguish, bringing me to the depth of despair and forcing me to once again face the devil, who was patiently waiting for me.

145

My parents are living in Sarasota, Florida, and my mother's finishing up her last round of radiation from her recent lumpectomy. At 8 p.m., I call them to let them know that there is a very strong possibility that Hunter has bone cancer.

The very next call is to Trevor. I chose that sequence intentionally. I knew that as soon as I told Trevor, he would break down—and I didn't feel strong enough to hold him and myself up at the same time. My parents gave me the fortitude I needed. *Don't get ahead of myself. Stay strong for Hunter. My fear will become his fear. Just focus on the one next action I need to take.*

Now we are back at the condo and Hunter is preoccupied with his video games. I make the call to Trevor. He knows the fear that comes with such news. He had been told twice in his life that he had cancer (the first time, he was only a year older than Hunter). He comes undone.

As parents, we do anything and everything possible to protect our kids and keep them safe and healthy. Trevor feels that his own genetics are the cause of Hunter's cancer and the crushing guilt of that is overwhelming. His addiction takes off once more, and the chaos begins.

The next several days are a blur of blood tests, MRI's, CAT scans, and a biopsy which confirms my worst fear: osteosarcoma, left tibia. They tell me there will be chemotherapy for three months, then surgery, then six more months of chemo. Friends could visit, but only if and when his white blood count is high enough that he wouldn't be susceptible to infection or illness. No more sports, no more school, no more parties. When you are 13 years old, those are the only things that matter.

When the news about Hunter hits our small town, we are immediately inundated with an outreach of love and support. Hunter's friends gather around him and fill his days with distractions and fun, while I focus on restructuring my responsibilities so I can take care of him. I am working full-time with my sales commissions being a large part of my income; I feel I have to work 40 or more hours every week to survive financially and keep my medical insurance which is more important now than ever before. In addition, I am halfway through an on-line master's program and, more than ever, I need to get to as many meetings as I can. My recovery needs to be as strong as ever.

My anxiety is high and emotions are raw. Too much to do. Too many decisions to make. My phone alerts me with text messages and phone calls non-stop. Friends, family, coworkers, teachers, doctors, nurses, appointments to be scheduled, tests to be done, constantly waiting on test results. Has it spread? What is his prognosis? WILL HE SURVIVE???

I wait alone, as patiently as possible, for the call—the call that will let me know if his cancer has spread, and I am starting to unravel.

I know I am a minute away from a drink or a drug. First call is to Kristen. No answer.

Next call is to Jen. She is crying, not knowing what to do or how to help. I end up consoling her because I can't stand to see her in pain, either. When I hang up, I realize that helping her has actually helped me and I am grateful for that.

There is a knock at my door. I open the door to a woman and a very tall teenager who has thinning hair and greyish skin.

She reaches out her hand. "Hi, I'm Liz, and this is my son, Robby."

And it hits me. Robby is a few years older than Hunter and was battling an extremely rare bone cancer which had metastasized to his lungs. In a flash, I recall the passing conversations around town. "Did you hear about Robby?" "Bone cancer, poor kid." "That poor family! I can't imagine what they are going through." I couldn't, either.

I give them both a quick hug and welcome them in. "I'm sorry to come unannounced," Liz says, "but I understand you are going to get a call today with Hunter's test results, and I was hoping I could keep you company until then."

I am flabbergasted at her generous offer of compassion and caring. I do not know her at all, but here she is, showing genuine concern for me and Hunter. I look over at the table where I had been sitting alone with only my phone for company. I motion for her to sit down.

Liz knew that I would need someone there if the tests revealed that the cancer had spread.

Robby makes his way upstairs to play video games with Hunter while Liz and I chat about everything that was happening and wait for the call.

She tells me that Robby is done with his treatment for the moment, so now they are waiting to see if the chemo, radiation, and multiple surgeries have been successful. His cancer is so rare that it has been reported only two other times. They had no protocol for treatment, so they are throwing everything at him and praying for the best.

Liz is absolutely beautiful. She has long blonde hair and blue eyes. She reminds me of an angel. Yet there is a palatable sadness that radiates from deep in her soul. She tries to push it away or cover it up, but I can see and feel it.

She knows her son will not win this war. She wants to believe with everything she has that he will, but she has been told the crude reality that his disease will eventually take his life. Sooner, rather than later.

The phone rings and startles us both. It is great news; the cancer has not spread. His chances of survival have just doubled, and I start to cry. I want to say that I am crying happy tears, but the reality is I am feeling an overwhelming sense of sadness and guilt, for Liz.

When Liz and Robby leave, I get in my car and drive. I need to get out of the condo, away from the emotions and confusion of it all. Hunter is happy to see me go and have some time alone.

I park in the church parking lot that will house an AA meeting in two hours. I sit in my car and pray until the meeting starts. *Please God, heal my son. Please don't let him die. Please, please, please...*

The topic of the meeting's discussion is "One Day at a time." Now, if that isn't God speaking to me, I don't know what is.

I am the first to raise my hand. "I'm Deb and I am an addict and alcoholic." I look around the room and into the faces of several people I have known for the last nine years. For the first time in a week, I feel safe.

"My son was diagnosed with bone cancer last week and I am falling apart," I begin. "I am so overwhelmed with things to do and decisions to be made that my head is spinning, and I am so scared, and I just don't know what to do. The doctors say this is a rare cancer that requires a brutal chemotherapy regimen, not to mention the 8-10 hours surgery he will need! His father can't handle this at all because of his history with cancer…he's drowning himself in weed and Percocets. Everyone is so devastated and sad that I end up consoling them because they don't know what to say. I am terrified that I am going to lose my job, my condo, and my health insurance if I can't work full time. But the worst part is I am so swamped with all of these worries that I haven't had a minute to focus on Hunter and his needs! How am I going to get through this?"

I am crying now, letting it all out. When someone gives me a tissue, I stop to look around and see the emotions of those around me. Many know Hunter from the times when I didn't have a babysitter, so he came to meetings with me. Those who never met him, know of him from the many times I spoke about him during my shares at a meeting.

The love I feel is so palatable in this room and I know without a doubt that I will find my strength and fortitude to get through this with the people in this church basement.

The rest of the hour-long meeting is spent with people opening up about traumatic events they have been through and how they survived it, sober. I am deeply touched and humbled to hear stories of the most horrific kinds—and the dignity and grace in which they were handled. "This program," a woman shares, "taught me that I could and would survive anything that comes my way without having to pick up a drink. There is nothing that God has presented me with that I haven't come through being stronger and smarter than I was before."

By the end of this meeting, I felt renewed. Something inside of me had come alive. My spirit was stronger, and I felt resilient, like I could take on anything.

I leaned on the program sayings that used to make my eyes roll: "easy does it" and "one day at a time" and, the all-important "let go and let God." I use every single slogan and 12-Step prayer to help me to make it through the next year. And that year would be full of the most challenging, heart breaking, gut wrenching, days of my life.

CHAPTER
14

Expect the Unexpected

It's time. Hunter starts his first round of chemotherapy at the children's hospital tomorrow. My parents have rented a nearby condo for a year so they can help. My employer was generously flexible with my work schedule and my customers were equally as kind, making sure orders were placed and new business came my way. The community rallied around us with multiple fund-raisers to help with the mountain of medical bills. With people's support and strength from my Higher Power, I can take a breath and focus on getting Hunter through this ghastly journey.

He starts his first Chemo IV with Trevor and me by his side. Trevor is nervous and sweating, pacing the floor, unable to sit still. We watch the IV bag with the vile orange substance drip the poison into my son's beautiful, healthy flesh. I sit still, looking around the room, wondering what we can bring in to make it more comfortable for him. We are told that he could be in this hospital room for about five days, depending on how quickly the chemo clears from his system and his white blood cells recover. Hunter is preoccupied on his phone, most likely sending out snap chats, which is okay with me. I want him to feel like a normal 13-year-old boy.

The IV bag is now empty and a whole other host of drugs will be administered—one for nausea, one for hydration, one to protect his heart and other organs from the damage that the toxic, heinous poison will cause, plus multiple others. This course of treatment is supposed to save his life, but there are short- and long-term costs to Hunter: the chemotherapy will cause him to be sterile, taking away his ability to have children outside of invitro fertilization. He and his future wife will have to undergo IVF with the sperm he now has stored on ice. I feel a sting of guilt. Did my desperate need and want for a child cause this misery? At the time, I had no way of knowing that Trevor carried a mutated gene which would be passed down to our kids, but even so, I can't help but feel I forced this calamity on him.

Before the administration of these drugs, the nurse sits down with Trevor and me and hands us a five-inch-thick binder filled with information on the medications our son will be getting in the hospital, along with the ones he will take at home. For over an hour, we go over every drug, their purpose, and the side effect. We touch on the "least likely to occur" side effects, which of course, are the life-threatening ones that no one wants to experience…or worse, have their child experience. I don't pay much attention to those as I am feeling confident in Hunters ability to cruise right through these treatments and be back to a healthy life in no time at all. I would quickly learn that my positive thoughts and faith would be tested every single day.

Six hours after the chemo cocktail has dripped into Hunter's veins, he is violently ill. Nothing is helping to stop the vomiting. He is given high doses of anti-nausea drugs through his IV, hydration to push the chemicals out, anti-anxiety medication to relax him. Nothing is working.

All we can do is comfort him as he dry-heaves every couple of minutes for eight hours. No sleep, no nourishment, no peace. His body aches from the spasms and he is wiped out. Now, we know that this is so much more powerful than we had believed it to be. I decide I need some prayer warriors.

I call every single person who has asked me over the preceding weeks, "What can I do?" and ask them to pray. Within 24 hours, there are prayer groups throughout the country and overseas, lifting him up, asking God to heal him, and to let his recovery be swift.

By day five he is feeling better and desperate to go home. The problem is that the chemo is not clearing from his body as quickly as we hoped, so five days turns into 10 days. No friends or visitors.

Just me and Trevor, who comes and goes throughout the day, leaving us to go God-knows-where to do God-knows-what. When he is in the room with us, he is nodding off or speaking in sentences that are nonsensical. I realize this is too much for him to bear and his escape is into the deep abyss of self-medicated numbness.

Hunter is frustrated and the reality of it all hits him. This will be a battle for his life and a war is raging against him. What we had hoped and expected did not come to fruition. The first round of poison kicks his ass and the ones that follow will nearly take his life.

We are finally home. Hunter's friends have decorated his door with "Welcome Home" signs and messages of love and hope. There is a steady friend stream into the house and up to his room to hang out. My parents are over, and we are putting a schedule into place. They will stay with Hunter during the day while I go to work. Trevor has gone off the grid, so I can't depend on him. He barely answers his phone, and when he does, it is easy to tell he is high. I have to work as much as possible to keep my income as well as feel some normalcy. I also need to get to a meeting. It's been two weeks, the longest I have ever gone without a meeting during my sobriety. Not a good idea.

We receive an outpouring of support and, thankfully, meal deliveries come regularly. I am astounded by the amount of people (some I know, most I do not) who have reached out. I see a side of humanity that makes my heart swell. The women in my recovery circle are in close contact every day, checking in and reminding me to get to a meeting. Jen is making sure I am always supplied with her famous chocolate chip cookies, and Kristen brings Hunter his favorite mac-and-cheese.

Our little condo is often filled with people desperate to help in a helpless situation. The love I am feeling allows for a moment of serenity and peace that I relish.

Now, two weeks later, we are checking into the hospital for his second round of chemotherapy. Although it's more dreaded before it starts than the first round, he tolerates this one better, and we are back home by the following week. Now his hair is beginning to fall out. Chunks of it. We are witness to the chemotherapy killing the healthy cells in his body, and I constantly remind myself and my son, that it is killing the cancer cells, too.

The third round is the last one before his limb salvation surgery. This time the effects hit him hard, and he is reeling. The vomiting won't stop, and we all feel helpless.

"Mom," he cries in between heaves, "please, I can't do this. Please, Mom, don't make me. Please. Make. It. Stop."

All I can do is rub his back and attempt in vain to comfort him. My heart is being ripped open and I feel a rage inside of me that I have never experienced.

When rest finally comes for him, I leave his room and feel a tremendous urge to scream and break something. I have to find a way to release this hatred in my heart. Instead, I pick up my phone and call Kristen. She answers in her happy voice, and I feel better already, until she starts the conversation with, "Hello lovey, Pete and I are just about to start a movie. Can I call you back?"

What I say is, "Sure." What I am thinking is, *ARE YOU FUCKING SERIOUS??!!*

She does not know the experience I was just coming out of, and I don't tell her, so she thinks nothing of dismissing me. For me, this just adds insult to injury. I am so, so frustrated about this situation, this familiar feeling of having no control over something in my life.

I stew in this for a while and let it eat at me. *How could she put watching a movie with Pete in front of MY needs? Doesn't she understand what I am going through? Doesn't she know how much I need her?*

No, she does not know. I am living in an entirely different world from my friends now. Not only can they not understand, but also, I do not want them witnessing the horror of this reality. I keep a brave face on so others can feel comfortable around me. I don't want to see worry or pain in their eyes, so I often reply to their inquiries about Hunter with: "He is doing well, chugging along, thank you for asking."

But with every moment of silence, the dark reality of the situation and my lack of processing it in a healthy way is starting to take a toll. I deny the feelings. I ignore the signs. I keep stuffing the darkness further and further inside. It is a pain I know well, but it's agonizing, nonetheless. I know I need to reach out and ask for help. I know what to do, I just don't do it. Instead, I isolate. That gives the beast a glimmer of hope that he can once again take me down.

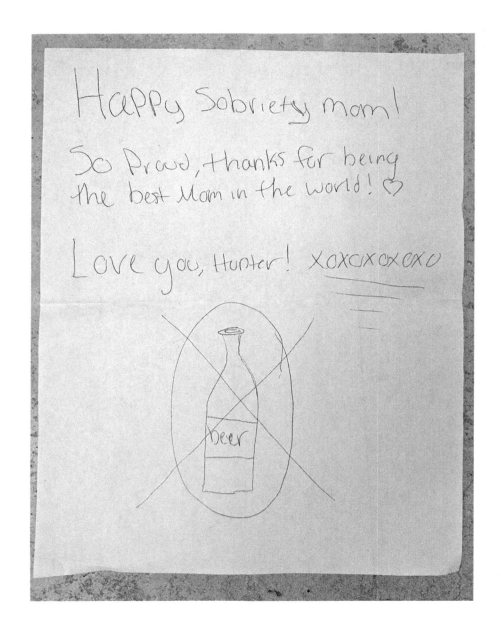

CHAPTER
15

Blessed to be a Drug Addict

"When is the surgery scheduled for?" a friend at a meeting asks.

"April twenty-fourth. I know it will take months for him to walk again...he'll need me a lot. I'll try to get to meetings, but obviously I can't leave him alone."

"Don't worry about that," she replies as she is walking away, "if you can't make it to us, then we will bring a meeting to you, wherever you are."

Wow. I am astounded at what people will do to help another addict. I have to ask myself if the tables were turned, would I do the same, or would I simply send well-wishes and continue on in my own little world. I feel ashamed that I can't honestly answer that question.

I look around the room, which is filled with women and men of all ages and backgrounds—doctors, teachers, plumbers, stay-at-home moms, students, retirees. There are at least 50 people at the meeting, each of them living their own life, fighting their battles, trying to make it through another day clean and sober.

I have learned that if I stay separated from the fellowship for too long, I become depleted, so I relish the recharge I am feeling. The energy in the church basement is high, with lots of chatter and laughter between friends. I feel my spiritual and emotional tank being filled. My fear of the unknown washes over me frequently during the day and keeps me up at night, but when I am here, in this church, with these folks, I am safe.

The topic of the meeting tonight is *acceptance*. Perfect.

I soak in everything that is shared and marvel at how resilient people are to unspeakable sufferings. I learn from those around me that life is not fair—unacceptable situations will confront us, but the sooner we accept what is being presented, the faster we can find a solution, which will allow room for peace and serenity.

This is my home, I am thinking, *these are my people, and despite the unacceptable reality of my son having cancer, I am abundantly blessed.*

CHAPTER
16

Bullet Holes and Titanium Rods

Hunter and I are out and about, stopping by friends and family for short visits, taking advantage of the freedom we have before tomorrow's surgery and his lengthy time in recovery. This is also a good way to keep my mind occupied and the dreadful "what if" thoughts at bay.

This surgery is major.

They are removing his left tibia and knee, replacing the bone with a titanium rod. I try to focus on the positives, like the fact that after the surgery his cancerous tumor will be out of his body, but I also know this is going to be a life-changing process of recovery and healing.

"Come on, kiddo," I say to Hunter. "It's time to head home, we have an early morning." I try to sound normal, but not too chipper. It's not like we need to get a good night's sleep before we head to Disney World, and Hunter doesn't need to have a phony layer of cheer spread on our reality. It would only reveal my underlying terror.

As we round the corner onto our road, I see a lot of police action in front of our garage. And there's a large truck with "Major Crime Unit" written on it. I watch enough *Law and Order* to know that Major Crimes only arrives at the scene if there is, well, a major crime, like a homicide.

Given that we live in a quiet, gated complex where most residents are retirees, I cannot imagine what is going down or why it is happening at our condo.

Hunter stays in the car as I speak to the sergeant, who calmly explains that my neighbor had attempted to kill her husband by shooting him. Fortunately, she missed. Unfortunately, the bullet went through their bedroom wall and exited out of the adjacent wall—which happens to be in MY bedroom.

My next-door neighbors, both in their seventies, are now down at the police station being charged with domestic violence and attempted murder. Everyone has their battles.

With all the commotion, it is well after midnight before sleep comes. It seems like only minutes later that I am hearing the alarm. It's 5 a.m. and I am jolted awake. One second later, it hits me. I have to get up, wake up Hunter, and keep an appointment for his life-altering surgery. It's going to be a long day.

The surgery takes over nine hours. I wait—each hour, an eternity.

He is moved to the ICU, where he will receive intensive care for three days. My parents and I are able to see him once he is settled. The sight of him takes my breath away. He is hooked up to several different machines, all beeping and flashing. The nurse is tending to them and explaining what each hanging bag contains and why. Hunter looks so fragile with his bald head propped up on several pillows, his face so pale. His leg is wrapped in a brace and propped up, making it look five times larger than the other. He is barely awake, yet moaning in pain.

"Mom," he cries, "it hurts!"

"I know honey, they are adjusting the pain meds."

I take a seat on his left side and my mom sits to his right. We sandwich him with love and comfort and do our best to keep it together.

Trevor is somewhere in the hospital...I have no idea where. He showed up to see Hunter off to the operating room, and that was the last I saw of him. I keep him updated throughout the day via text, but have yet to see him. When he finally does show up, he is jittery and sweating. I know he is coming off of something, but I can't be bothered with that now.

It's three days later and Hunter is moved to a room on the oncology floor of the children's hospital, where he will spend the next few weeks learning to walk with his new leg.

He is getting an IV of Dilaudid, but is still constantly complaining about the pain.

"By now he should be on oral pain meds, but he is still asking for more of the IV, which doesn't make sense to me," his surgeon says. "He shouldn't be in that much pain at this point. I will give him another day before we switch him over."

I know immediately what is happening. He has gotten a taste of the opioids and the switch has been turned on. The beast is coming for my son.

The next day I sit down with Hunter's oncologist.

"We need to discuss a pain management plan for Hunter that does not include narcotics," I begin. "It's important that you and your team know that I am a recovering addict and Hunter's dad is an active addict. We both became addicted to pain meds. Hunter doesn't have a chance against this disease if we don't do something now."

The doctor looked at me for a minute and then says, "We don't worry about kids at this age becoming addicted to pain meds. Hunter has just endured a massive surgery and he will be in pain that requires narcotics. However, he will be weaned off as soon as possible. At this juncture, we want to make sure he is comfortable."

"Well, of course I don't want him in pain either, but please be aware what his genetic makeup is with regards to opioids," I respond.

"Noted," he replies.

For the next several weeks, it's one issue after another, from Hunter developing drop foot (loss of nerve function in his foot), to multiple wound infections and intestinal issues from the multitude of narcotics he is taking. He suffers through every single medication side effect, even the "less common" ones.

I feel like I am living inside of a pressure cooker, ready to explode. Every minute of every single day is spent trying to resolve some medical issue or crisis. It seems the only time he is peaceful is when he is hooked up to an opioid IV. This scares the shit out of me.

Since the surgery, I live at the hospital, day and night. I am running really low on patience and tolerance. I need to go to a meeting desperately, but with everything going on at the hospital, I just don't feel like I can leave for even an hour.

And then, as if on cue, my phone rings. Under normal circumstances I would not answer—too tired and stressed to chat, but for some reason I do. I walk out to the hallway to take the call.

"Hey, Deb," my friend Betsy says, with her midwestern drawl, "How are you doing?"

"Not great, honestly," I say, "it's a shit show here and I am coming unraveled." I start to cry.

"Wow, I am so sorry. Have you been able to get to a meeting at all?" she asks

"No, and that's part of the problem," I say. "I just can't get away long enough. It seems like every hour there is something else happening with my son that I need to be here for."

"Well, then," Betsy states, "it's a good thing we are bringing a meeting to you!"

I turn around and there are a handful of friends from AA walking toward me. Oh, how I need this! They envelop me in their arms and let me cry my eyes out. This feels good. The pressure has been released from the cooker.

We sit in the visitor's lounge and hold a 12-Step meeting. I am in the presence of strong, sober women who share their own life struggles and victories. For that one hour, there is no particular focus on me or Hunter. It's just everyday life, like it used to be.

By the time they leave, I feel renewed. What had been so dark and heavy is light. I'm ready to take on whatever comes my way.

I open the door to Hunter's room and there is Trevor. He had crawled into bed with Hunter, forcing him to move his leg, and promptly passed out. Hunter is clearly uncomfortable, but I'm not surprised he didn't say anything for fear of hurting Trevor's feelings. Immediately the angst and upset that I had just shed pour over me again.

"TREVOR!!" I shout as I push on him, "TREVOR!" No response. I know from past experiences that when he is passed out from opioids, there is no waking him up.

"Mom, my leg," Hunter whispers in destress. If Trevor rolls one inch over, he'll be directly on top of Hunter's wound.

I walk to the sink, fill a cup with water and pour it on Trevor's face. Fortunately, this wakes him. Unfortunately, he is enraged and lunges out of bed at me. The force of his movement causes pressure on Hunters leg, and he yells out in pain. The scream is enough to get Trevor's attention and snaps him back into reality.

"You're such a bitch," he says and leaves the room without even a nod to Hunter.

I look at Hunter and can see he feels guilty about the scene that just played out. I assure him that none of this is his fault. I ache with empathy for his pain, but also feel gratitude that I am in recovery. Thank God! If I wasn't, Hunter wouldn't have either parent to depend on. Another gift of sobriety.

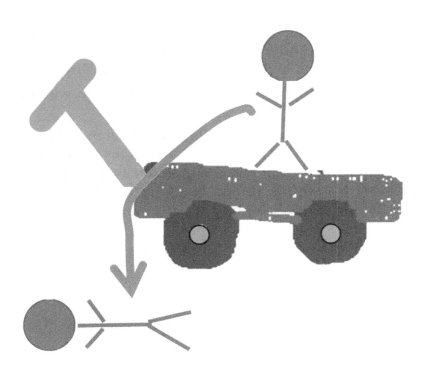

CHAPTER
17

Off the Grid and Off the Wagon

I know from Robby and other kids who have traveled this road ahead of Hunter that the next several months will be brutal. I just had no idea how brutal, and on how many levels.

It's been a month since Hunter's surgery and our brief reprieve from chemotherapy treatments is over. It's the weekend before he starts his next round and Jen has a party for Hunter and all of his friends. It is a perfect night. Hunter is surrounded by nearly 30 of his classmates and close friends. Jen, Kristen, and I stay upstairs and catch up on all the latest news in town. It has been a few weeks since any kind of real conversation with Kristen and I'm anxious to hear about what is new at the women's meeting we used to regularly attend.

"So, tell me how everyone is doing! Did Stacy get her one-year chip last week?" I ask, excited to hear everything.

"I don't know, actually," Kristen says, not looking me in the eyes. "I haven't been at that meeting in a while. I think I only went once since you were there."

"How come?" I ask, surprised. That had been a staple meeting for her since she had gotten clean 15 years prior.

"I don't know. I just needed a break. Plus, Pete and I have been really busy with the kids' sports and activities. It's tough because we are in different towns and every night there is some game or practice going on."

I am flushed with irritation. I had felt Kristen and I disconnecting over the past few months, but I thought maybe it was because she was trying to not overwhelm me with calls and texts. I had mentioned to her that it gets overwhelming when my phone is constantly blowing up. Now I know it was not that. It was because she was putting all her time and energy into her relationship with Pete, her new man.

"So, are you getting to any meetings?" I ask.

"I have been to a few, but honestly, everyone there is annoying me. It's the same people telling the same stories over and over. I end up leaving feeling aggravated, so I am taking a break."

"Okay" is all I say. What I want to ask is, "Are you taking a break from me too? Cause we don't talk much these days." I don't say anything, not the time or the place.

"Help!" That night I dream that I am being sucked down into quicksand and I am screaming for help when I see Kristen and Pete walking toward me. I reach my hand up so she can pull me out, but she just looks at me and says, "I can't help you. Pete and I are going to the beach."

I wake up knowing that our friendship has shifted, and I can no longer rely on her like I had for so many years.

CHAPTER
18

Suffocating

For the first time, I find myself wondering if my son will live through this ordeal, no longer sure that he'll survive both the damaging effects of cancer and its traumatizing treatment.

We are back at the hospital and the chemotherapy has started dripping into his veins. Now that the surgery is over, he will be blasted with chemo every three weeks for several months. The drugs will kill every cancer cell along with healthy cells. It's a catch 22—can't kill the bad without bringing down the good.

The vomiting has started and will not stop for several days. His hair is completely gone, eye lashes and brows as well. He has lost so much weight that when he lurches over the puke bucket to vomit, you can see every bone in his spine. The wounds from his surgery are starting to become infected, and he has canker sores on all his soft tissue from his mouth to his rectum. His white blood count is becoming dangerously low, and we are all desperately worried about any infection invading him.

He looks up at me after dry heaving into the stupidly pink plastic vomit bucket. His skin is grey and his eyes are dull, sitting in sockets of black. "I can't do this anymore, Mom."

For the first time since his diagnoses, I am terrified. I have witnessed his spirit dying along with any flicker of hope he has been holding onto.

I suddenly feel an enormous weight on my chest, and I can't catch my breath. I. can't. breathe.

I walk into the bathroom so as not to alarm Hunter, who has now disappeared into his favorite position of being completely engulfed under the covers. His little cocoon.

I try to take a deep breath, but I can't. The weight on my chest is getting heavier and I am starting to panic. Just then, a nurse walks in the room to check Hunter's vitals and I wave her into the bathroom where she sees I am in trouble. "Sit down" she commands, "I'll be right back."

I have no choice. I sit on the toilet seat and gasp for air. She comes back with a paper bag and says in that soft but firm voice that the best nurses everywhere have, "Breath into this, slowly." She rubs my back as she guides me though breathing until my lungs open up and I feel the relief of air filling them.

I start to cry. "What was THAT?" I ask, sobbing.

"That," she responds, "was a panic attack. You, my friend, need to give yourself a break and practice some self-care. I know this is a lot, but you are no good to him if you aren't taking care of yourself."

"I'm his mom. He needs me to be here."

"Yes, he needs you, but trust me," the nurse says, "he sees and feels your stress and that is not doing him any favors. Let us take care of him medically and you call in your parents or other family to be here for his emotional needs for the next few days. If anything happens where he needs you, we will call you."

At this juncture, Trevor is useless. I can barely get him on the phone, and when he does show up, he is such a mess you can't understand a word he is saying before he passes out, either on the couch or on the floor in the hallway. The hospital is getting ready to refuse his visitation right because of his behavior.

I hear Hunter calling for me. We walk out of the bathroom to find him sitting up in bed. "What is going on? Why were you guys in the bathroom?" he asks.

"I just needed a minute, honey," I reply.

"Mom, why don't you just go home," he says. The nurse was right. He knows I am coming undone and to see me like this is only making him feel worse. He would often apologize for having cancer, seeing the emotional toll it was taking. I want desperately for him to see only my strength and virtue, but Hunter could always read my moods and emotions better than I can myself. I can never hide or fake an emotion around him. We are *that* connected.

"No, that's okay. I want to stay." I lie. I am so emotionally and physically spent that I just want to go home and crawl into my big, comfy bed and sleep for days. But I feel I can't leave him now. He is too fragile.

"Whatever," he says, sounding aggravated. He slides back into his cocoon.

Five minutes later, the doctor arrives to inform us that Hunter's white blood count is too low for him to remain in an open room, so he will be going into an isolation room until further notice. No visitors allowed for the next 48 hours. This includes parents.

Apprehensively, I say goodbye to Hunter and leave the hospital. I've never felt so emotionally and physically exhausted. I get into my car, sit down, and start bawling. Seeing him so sick and watching the hope in him disappear scares me to death, and I ask out loud to God, "Is my son going to die?" I wait for an answer, but none comes. I do have a tiny flash of realization that it was divine intervention that gave me a guilt-free exit to leave the hospital and recover my own strength.

I get myself together and start my half-hour drive home. After a few minutes, my phone rings. I am surprised and happy to see it is Kristen calling. We haven't been speaking on a regular basis, but at this moment, I don't care. I desperately need to unload and talk through the day I've had.

"Hello there! I'm so glad you're calling. I have had a helluva day and could use an ear," I say.

"Oh, no!" Kristen says, "I'm so sorry, honey, tell me what's going on!"

Just hearing her voice—my dear friend, my sponsor—makes me feel a little better. I spill it all out: every piece of news, our challenges, and my feelings and emotions; my fear about Hunter not making it through these treatments; what he said, his loss of hope, and how sick he looks; my panic attack. She listens patiently, offering me support and empathy. That's all she can provide, but it's profoundly helpful.

"So," I go on, feeling some renewed energy and relief getting that off my chest, "what's new with you? I feel like we haven't spoken in so long! Tell me everything."

"Well…there is a reason I am calling you," Kristen says.

"Okay, what's up?" I'm not sure if I should be worried or just curious.

"So…I wanted to let you know that I decided a few weeks ago to start drinking."

Silence. Shock. Disbelief. Confusion. I think I may need to pull the car over and stop. She continues, "I know this is a shock to you, but I want you to know that I am okay now, but if things get out of control, I know where to go, so don't worry about me."

I cannot begin to wrap my head around what she is telling me. I am too stunned to utter a word.

Finally, I say, "So, you decided a few weeks ago…does that mean you are still thinking about it?"

"No, I drank a few weeks ago."

"But—wait." Head spinning. "Why?"

"I always struggled with thinking I was an alcoholic. I mean, I know I am an addict, but I feel like I can handle alcohol," she answers.

"I'm confused," I say. "This is the exact excuse everyone says when they go out and you always told me it's total bullshit. You said that is the disease talking, that no addict can use mind altering substances in a healthy way."

"Listen," Kristen says, "I know it's confusing, but I promise I have everything under control, and if I feel like I am losing it, you will be the first person I call."

I know there is no talking her out of it, or changing her mind with some 12-Step slogan or heartfelt concern. I am too spent to try, so we hang up.

Driving the rest of the way home, the shock is wearing off and I am becoming more and more furious with her. I keep thinking,

How could she do this right now? I am fighting the biggest battle of my life, and she has just stepped out of the ring.

As an addict, it's so typical for her to not think about how her decisions affect others. And as an addict myself, it's so typical for me to think about how this is about me. *I have never needed her more and she has decided that Pete and beer are more important than supporting her best friend! How fucking selfish can one person be?!*

I have not only lost my sponsor, but I have also lost my best friend—both of whom I need now more than ever. *She had 15 years of clean time! Her whole life is in AA and, what? Now she just cuts off everything and everyone? How the fuck does this happen?!* Angry tears sting my eyes.

By the time I arrive home, I am a jumble of emotions—sad, exhausted, confused, worried, resentful, furious, and highly agitated. I walk up to my bedroom on auto pilot and into my bathroom. I take out every single bottle of Hunter's pain meds and lay them out on my bed, taking inventory of each one:

Percocet
Oxycodone
Methadone
Dilaudid
Tramadol
Gabapentin
Fentanyl patches
Benzodiazepine
Ativan
Xanax

A whole pharmacy of all my favorites at my disposal. Just one, little, pill will make all this pain disappear. Just *one little pill* will allow me to sleep soundly for once. Just *one little pill* will make me not give a shit about Kristen or anything going on in my life. Just *one little pill* will make it all go away.

The powerful magnetic pull of the pills is so intense, I scoop up all the bottles and hold them to my chest. I sit, cross-legged on my bed, eyes closed, rocking back and forth, feeling the familiar comfort of my old friends. Just imagining how I was about to feel once I took one pill gave me such a rush of euphoria that I laugh out loud. I am overjoyed with anticipation.

My little Boston Terrier, Teeka, jolts awake at my outburst and jumps up onto the bed, curious to know what my excitement is all about. She makes her way over to me and sniffs the bottles I am clutching. She looks at me, and then nuzzles her way onto my lap, demanding a snuggle, which forces me to put the bottles down. Once she is between me and the pills, I snap out of my trance.

I am absolutely terrified that I've come so close to relapsing. I begin to shake and sob uncontrollably. I slide off my bed onto my knees.

For the first time in my life, I really surrender to God. I don't ask for a favor or help. I don't beg or plead for something to go my way. I simply surrender.

"Please, God," I pray, "I cannot fight this battle without you. You are in control...I see that now. I no longer want to live a life directed by anyone or anything besides you. Tonight, I fully surrender my life and my will to you. Please forgive my sins and take away my shortcomings so nothing blocks my connection to you and the Holy spirit. I ask this through Jesus Christ, amen."

I cry my way through the words and when I am done, I fall fast asleep, fully clothed on my bed, next to ten bottles of pills. Unopened.

19

The Turning Point

My eyes fly open. It's dark and the only sound is my phone ringing. I realize it's only 4 a.m. and Hunter is calling me. "Mom?" His voice is cracking, and my heart jumps into my throat.

"Hi, honey," I say, trying to sound calm. "Are you okay?"

My mind is so foggy from sleep, I have to think about where he is and where I am. As I sit up, I knock several pill bottles off the bed. The sound of the pills rattling as they the hit the floor makes my stomach lurch.

"Are you on your way?" he asked.

"No, love, it's only four in the morning. I can't get in until eight. Plus, the doctor told us yesterday that there aren't any visitors allowed while you are in isolation."

"Mom, please," he cries, "I need you here. I'm scared and my leg really hurts. There is something wrong. Please come."

I am now wide awake, and panic is setting in. "It's okay, honey, everything is going to be okay," I say, trying to convince myself more than him. "Page your nurse and let me talk to her when she gets to your room."

I hear him buzzing his nurse and asking her to come to his room. "Hi, Hunter," I hear through the phone, "what do you need?"

"My mom is on the phone and wants to talk to you."

"Tell her I will call her from the phone out here," she responds. A minute later, I am talking to Diane, Hunter's favorite night nurse.

"What's happening?" I begin. "He wants me to come in, says he is scared."

"Well," she says, "he has had a tough night. He spiked a fever and was upset because we wouldn't call you. It's down now, but he is still uncomfortable."

"Why didn't you call me about the fever?" I ask, feeling annoyed.

"Because I knew you would want to come down here, but we couldn't allow you into his room." She continues to explain that while he is in isolation, you cannot go in and out of his room because of the risk of infection (and his body's inability to handle any germs at all). Once you're in, you stay in, but if you leave the room, you cannot go back in.

The bottom line is no one is allowed to see him until he is transferred back to his room on the floor, and that could be days.

I hang up with Diane and give myself a minute before calling Hunter back with the news that he will be alone to fight his battle for a few days. *God, help him.*

I start picking up all the pill bottles. With each one I touch; I feel more and more uncomfortable and unsettled. I toss them all in the back of my linen closet and shut the door. The bottles I had held close like long-lost friends the night before suddenly repulse me. I feel repelled from them like a snake from fire, which is exactly what the Big Book of AA says will happen when you live a sober life. Once again, the promises of recovery are coming true.

Now, in this moment, I know that I will never have to turn to drugs or alcohol to get through a painful or traumatizing situation. They are no longer required to dull pain or distract me from life's hard days.

I had known this in the past, but never actually *felt* it. This was the first real test for me, and I came within an inch of failing, but I leaned into God, and He was there. My prayer of surrender the previous night changed everything for me. This is the second time since being in recovery that I experienced how God works through prayer, and I desperately want to experience more.

I call Hunter back and explain to him why he can't have any visitors. He sobs on the phone and my heart breaks into a million pieces.

When we hang up, I get on my knees and ask God to help me through this. I need His strength and comfort so I can help Hunter. I pray to God to give Hunter strength and perseverance through the tough days. I know instinctually there will be more.

I just would have never imagined how many, and the circumstances that would arise.

———————◇———————

Since I can't visit Hunter in his isolated room, I take the next few days to work on myself. I go to two or three meetings every day. I connect with friends I haven't spoken to in a while, and I rummage through my storage to find my long-lost Bible. I know I own a Bible, and I also know I have never read it. Now, something within me is yearning to be closer to God and I figure that reading the Bible would be a good place to start.

I was wrong. Reading the Bible is confusing to me and makes me feel even further away from God. So, I try what I am much more comfortable and familiar with, turning on Netflix and starting to watch the series, *The Bible*.

Watching the series is wonderful. It is a perfect way for me to get acquainted with the Bible and the scriptures without becoming intimidated or discouraged by the written word.

In addition to learning about God and Jesus, I also become engrossed with learning about the afterworld and what happens when we die. I figure that if Hunter passes away, I want to know exactly what he would experience. I read and watch everything I can on near-death experiences, spirit guides, and angels. I talk with friends, holy men, psychics, therapists, and anyone else who will share their thoughts, feelings, and knowledge on the subject. It becomes a private obsession. I *need* to know where he would be if he died.

I find great comfort in hearing stories of people crossing over and feeling extraordinary love. No pain or sadness. No anxiety or fear. No broken body. Just an abundance of peace and love.

Their recalling of meeting Jesus is remarkable and gives me an extraordinary sense of internal peace whenever I read about these events. Somehow, I instinctively know I am being called to learn more about and build a relationship with God.

Inexplicably, I start to feel, think, and *know* that Hunter will win the war against cancer. To look at him, you would never put your money on his survival. He is not responding well to the treatments, and his leg is constantly infected. However, I am regularly receiving a calm, firm, and peaceful energy from *somewhere and something.* No matter what is thrown at me, I am able to handle it by leaning into my growing relationship with God. The message is clear; the war will be won. And, there will be many battles ahead for me to face with enough faith and belief in God for the both of us.

Another message comes through loud and clear; now, more than ever, I must nurture my recovery. If I do not remain clean and sober, there will be no possibility of me helping Hunter through the enormous challenges that are coming his way.

Prayer time, 12-Step meetings, and daily connections with other women in recovery are non-negotiable, regardless of my time constrictions. These give me strength and the sense that Hunter and I will get through this, one day at a time.

CHAPTER
20

The First to Fly Away

Cancer doesn't care how old or young you are.

We would lose Robby and the reality of cancer taking the life of a teenager would hit hard. Cancer doesn't consider your age: if it intrudes, it can take you down. The disease of addiction is the same. No one is safe, and money can't buy your life.

Robby was 19 years old when he died. Even though we knew the inevitable would happen, his passing still crushes our hearts.

He and Hunter had only known each other for two and a half years when God called for him, but they created a bond that could never be replaced. Robby treated Hunter like he was his little brother and always checked on him when he knew Hunter was about to undergo a chemo treatment or surgery.

When the time of his last days became clear, Robby's parents asked that visitors be limited to immediate family only, so I was surprised when Liz called and asked if I could bring Hunter to the hospital to visit Robby. "He is asking for Hunter," she said quietly, "is there a chance you can drive him down?"

"Absolutely," I replied, "we will be right there."

Not knowing what was happening, or why Robby was specifically asking to see Hunter, we raced to the hospital and within a half hour we were at his room. Robby was in palliative care by now, so he was being kept comfortable with medication. He was sleeping when we arrived but woke up soon after. He tried his best to sit up but didn't have the strength, so he motioned for Hunter to come closer and put out his fist for a fist pump like they had shared hundreds of times before. With all his strength, he mustered up the words, "Hey bud, how did the surgery go?"

I stood there, astonished. Hunter had been in the hospital a week earlier to have a surgery on his leg where a stubborn infection had grown, and antibiotics were not able to kill it off.

How in the world did Robby remember that? He had been in the hospital for several weeks at that point, fighting for his life. I couldn't imagine that he would be able to retain and recall that information, yet there he was, with only days left in his own life, checking to make sure Hunter was okay.

That is who Robby was. A beautiful soul who simply could not have peace in his heart until he saw Hunter one last time. Seeing Robby that day and being able to say goodbye gave us both a tremendous sense of comfort which I will always be grateful for.

Missing his friend and not knowing where to channel his feelings, Hunter decides the best way to deal with the pain is to create something positive. He organizes a charity golf tournament in Robby's name. Years later, the tournament is still going strong, raising and donating thousands of dollars to the Oncology Department at the Connecticut Children's Medical Center.

Over the past three months, the doctors have been trying to cure a staph infection in Hunter's leg. Nothing has worked. Hunter receives punch-in-the-gut news: there is nothing more the medical team can do. His left leg will be amputated above the knee.

Like any loss in our lives, Hunter processes this information in stages. First, denial, then anger, and finally, acceptance. To look at your child and come to terms with the fact that he will no longer have two legs takes a huge adjustment on my part. I brought this beautiful child into the world with 10 fingers and 10 toes, free to run and play, kick and climb. That was always how I pictured him.

My heart breaks, thinking of how difficult simple tasks will be for him once he has the operation. Will he ever run again? Ski? Play any sports? How will he get around if he doesn't have his prosthetic leg on? The "what if" game is reeling nonstop in my mind. And then the guilt sets in…again. Is he suffering in this life because I forced his birth by doing invitro fertilization? Is he having to endure agony because of our selfish decision to have a child?

Fear kicks in. More like terror. How am I going to pay for a $90,000 prosthetic leg? Insurance covers a portion; however, the remaining balance will put me even further into the stranglehold of debt I am already struggling to manage.

Once word makes its way around our community, friends, family and even strangers come together once again to help. Donations are made, fundraisers are held, and Hunter's cousin Max sets up a GoFundMe page. These remarkable acts of kindness and generosity are just one more sign from God that I am not facing these trying times alone.

The donations add up to enough to pay for the prosthetic and some outstanding medical bills. Again and again, I am blessed to see the miracles God provides. There is no denying His presence in my life, in Hunter's life, in the lives of all of His children.

The amputation is scheduled and within a week it will be over. I now have a new obsession that I can't seem to move past: what will they do with Hunter's leg once it is amputated? "Do you just throw it away?" I ask the surgeon. I can tell he is surprised by my question, but not necessarily shocked. I had insisted on seeing pictures of the previous operations on Hunter, so I would know what the implanted devices looked like and where they were placed in his leg. I want to know how his tendons, ligaments, and muscles will be reattached after the metallic knee and tibia are inserted. The surgeon obliges, and would later walk me through the photos, explaining everything that took place.

For me, knowing the process helps me to accept what is happening. When I asked about what would happen to his leg, it was so I could envision the procedure and come to terms with it. The surgeon explains that the leg will, in fact, be disposed of with other hospital organic waste to be cremated—and no, he would not take a photo of the amputation.

I am fine with that, but cannot move past the anger I feel, knowing that part of my son is going to be removed and thrown away. It enrages me, and I let everyone who will listen know how appalled I am. "They just cut it off and burn it with the trash!" I huff at whatever poor soul dares to ask how I am doing.

I sit in that anger for days, until a good friend from AA suggests that perhaps I am projecting my anger about the actual amputation onto the hospital's disposal protocol. "I mean, what are they supposed to do with it, give it back to you?" she asks.

This makes me laugh out loud and I finally come to my senses. She is absolutely correct. I was so angry about everything—his cancer diagnosis, losing Robby, and then the ultimate slap in the face, the life-altering amputation. I didn't know where to direct that anger, so I aimed it at the hospital waste disposal department. In my crazy brain, that made sense.

Hunter makes it through the surgery just fine. It's a few days later and he is getting up to take his first step without the use of his left leg. My friend Dave and I witness this and hear him say (to my delight), "This is the first time in months I don't have any pain."

And I think, *Me too, kiddo, me too.* His pain was my pain.

I thank God for seeing Hunter through another surgery and pray that this will be the end of his suffering. "Please, God, let this be his last battle."

What I hear back is not what I was hoping for. I hear, "There is still more to come." *Wait,* I think. *Did I hear that or say it in my head? I must have said it to myself. But, why? Why would I think such a negative thought?* I refuse to believe what I had heard and chalk it up to the devil getting in my head again, trying to bring me down.

CHAPTER
21

A Loss Like No Other

"Thanks for dinner, Mom," Hunter says as he carries his plate into the kitchen, balancing himself on one leg and crutches. I hold my breath, watching him as he maneuvers around with a half-full, breakable plate in his hands. Instinctively, I want to step in to help and take it from him, but I don't. I know he needs to learn to do these daily tasks on his own. And he doesn't need his mom acting like he is helpless.

It has been a few months since the amputation, and although he has a prosthetic to wear, the pain of wearing it can sometimes be too much, kind of like breaking in a new pair of shoes but on a much larger scale. He is slowly getting used to it, as I too am getting used to rounding a corner to see a "leg" leaning against the wall.

My phone is unusually active, but I ignore the pings, enjoying quiet, after-dinner time with Hunter and my boyfriend, Kevin.

Another call comes through. I see I have missed calls from Trevor's sister Carolyn and now his brother Grant is calling. I assume they are calling to ask how Hunter is doing, which is not unusual. I pick up the phone.

"Hey, Grant! How are you?"

"He's gone," Grant says, sobbing.

"What? Who?" I ask, truly confused.

"Trevor! He stopped breathing and they couldn't save him! He's dead!" Grant is crying so hard I can barely understand him, let alone process what he is telling me.

I turn around to see Hunter next to me asking, "What's up?" He can tell by my face that something terrible has happened. I have no time to figure out a graceful way to tell him that his father has just passed away.

"Grant, I will call you back." I hang up and look at Hunter, dumbfounded.

"Mom! WHAT HAPPENED?"

"Honey, sit down."

"NO! TELL ME!!" he demands.

I have no time to prepare. No time to soften the blow. I am suffocating.

"Your dad passed away," I tell him, not knowing what else to say.

Hunter is barely an arm's length from me. He is about a foot taller than me, standing with crutches, balancing on one leg. His hair has grown back thick and full, and his skin is no longer pale. He has come so far in the last year, physically and emotionally, but this may be what breaks him. I watch his face become contorted.

He sits down, throwing his crutches across the room. I jump at the noise of the metal hitting the hardwood floor. His hands are holding his head, and he screams, "WHAT THE FUCK!?!?" and "NO! NO! NO!" over and over.

Nothing comes to me to say or do. I'm stunned at the news, but only focused on my dear son and his pain. I know he must get it out and I let him. I have learned over the past years that when he is faced with distressing news, I need to give him physical and emotional space. He sits quietly, mind spinning, as I stand in the middle of the room, in the same place and position as when I answered the phone. I am frozen in place, unable to move.

"What happened?" he finally asks.

"I don't know the whole story, but from what I gathered from Uncle Grant, he had heart failure."

"But I just saw him yesterday and he seemed fine! What the fuck!?!?" He punches at his head with his fists. Confusion is still driving his emotions.

"I don't know, honey, I am so sorry. I will call Carolyn and find out what happened."

Hunter insists that I place the call on speaker phone so he can hear for himself. I do what he asks. I know my 17-year-old son has been through so much, he has maturity way beyond his years. I understand that for him to process this devastating news, he needs the entire story of what happened from someone who was there.

Carolyn answers immediately and is matter-of-fact in her recall of events. Trevor has been living in his parent's guest house while undergoing chemo treatments since his cancer returned, so that is where he was discovered. I can tell Carolyn has taken control, so her parents don't have to. She is strong and will carry us all through. I am grateful to her for this and always will be.

"He was complaining of pain in his leg when the visiting nurse arrived today," she begins, "so the nurse told us to check on him as soon as we were home from work. Nana and I found him on the floor. He was barely breathing, so I gave him CPR until the ambulance arrived, but it was too late. I am so sorry, Hunter."

We hang up the phone and I ask if he wants to take a ride to his grandparents to be with everyone. "No, I want to be alone." He walks up to his room where I hear him wailing for hours.

I sit down on the stairs, stunned, head in hands. I'm too shocked to cry for the man I married and had a son with. I know I will mourn for him, but right now, I only think of Hunter.

"Hey, babe...you okay?" A voice startles me.

I look up and see Kevin standing there. When the call came in, Kevin was considerate, leaving the house for a walk, giving us some space. I have never been so happy to have another person with me than at this moment. We have only been dating for six months, and during that time, Kevin has witnessed my life as a seesaw between challenges and chaos. Add on the death of Hunter's dad and I thought he would have run for the hills.

"I can't believe this is happening," I say quietly to Kevin. "I just don't know how he is going to deal with this on top of everything else he has been through."

"Give him space and time. He will be okay. That kid is resilient as hell."

The next morning, Hunter comes downstairs dressed and ready for school.

"Hey, kiddo," I say. "I called you out of school. You don't have to be back there until next week."

"I want to go," he says. "I don't want to sit around here bored all day."

"Okay, I get it."

He hugs me, tells me he loves me, and goes off to school. I guess he is even more resilient than I thought.

Trevor's life was a rollercoaster of addiction and untreated mental health disorders. He tried many times to pull himself out of the chaotic lifestyle that comes with addiction, and fought hard to overcome the demons that battled inside of him. During the last few months of his life, he spent time in a court-ordered rehab center, where he managed to stay clean. For the first time in Hunter's life, he was able to get to know his dad. They spent day after day together and my heart was bursting with gratitude and happiness for them and their newfound relationship. Hunter was seeing the *real* Trevor, the man I married and knew would be an amazing father.

After Trevor left rehab, a visit to his doctor would reveal that his reoccurring colon cancer was back and had metastasized. Hunter would often drive him to and from his doctor and chemo appointments, allowing them hours together. Although not the most pleasant of circumstances, Hunter enjoyed their time together and learned who his dad really was. It was a gift and blessing to them both.

Trevor and I were able to make amends and grant forgiveness to each other. Now he is gone and I feel fortunate that so much had healed between us. I am just shy of my twelfth year of sobriety. I made peace with the events of our past long ago, with the help of the fellowship and my connection to God. I have no room in my heart or head for anger or resentment towards Trevor, or anyone else, for that matter.

When I look back at our marriage, I can see clearly what caused Trevor to change so dramatically in such a short period of time. A few months before Hunter's birth, Trevor went for his yearly colonoscopy. He had been diagnosed at the tender age of 14 with colon cancer, which is highly unusual. Since his case was so rare, his doctors wanted him to get checked yearly, and so he did. This procedure, however, was not like the others. This time, there was a tumor in his colon and the tests showed the cancer had spread to part of his small intestines. He would need surgery to remove the cancerous growths.

Up until that very moment, our lives consisted of picking out countertops and flooring for the new condo we just purchased and praying daily that it would be ready in time for our baby's arrival. We had so much to look forward to and all our dreams were coming true.

However, when the news of the cancer hit, something inside of Trevor just snapped. He was convinced he was going to die, and his moods would fluctuate between intense anger and unbearable sadness.

Of course, he survived the surgery and physically healed in the expected time, however, he was never himself again. The amount of pain medications prescribed seemed unlimited. It was a good three months after the surgery that they cut him off. Right around the time I came home from the hospital with our son and a bottle of Percocet.

What we came to find out, was that Trevor experienced a bi-polar episode with the diagnosis of cancer. Between the stress of that news and the propensity of an addiction to pain meds, he didn't have a chance against the addiction.

Most of us who witnessed his erratic behavior did not know enough about either disease to intervene and get him the proper help he desperately needed. My way of dealing with it followed the "if you can't beat 'em, join 'em" philosophy, so that's what I did, and we all know how that ended up.

Hunter is mourning his father in a healthy way. He also is thankful for the last few months they spent together and knows, fully and completely, how much his dad loved him. Regardless of the events and circumstances of our past, I never doubted how much Trevor adored his son. Thank God Hunter learned that truth...nothing can take that from him.

Another hard truth strikes me; I am Hunter's only parent. If I go off the rails and back to drugs, he will have the inconceivable burden of having an addicted mother and dead father. I commit to even more meetings and self-care rituals to ensure that won't happen.

CHAPTER
22

My Beautiful Dragonfly

When your child is sick and spends more than half of his life at the hospital, you end up meeting other families who are walking the same road through hell. Some kids are close to the end of their treatment, others have just begun, and still more children are there due to a reoccurrence of their disease. Robby was one of these souls, and so is Hunter's new friend, Kyla.

Hunter, Robby, and Kyla were all close in age, so they found themselves hanging out a lot, both in the hospital and when they were all lucky enough to be home at the same time. The bond between kids and young adults who are battling life-threatening illness is unbreakable. They have a respect and regard for life that most adults have not mastered. During treatment, these kids wake up every day wondering if it will be their last. The reality of how fragile life is strikes at them every minute.

I have come to love these brave young souls. Their perseverance and determination to live is extraordinary, and their friendship is indestructible. There is no place I would rather be than with them. They inspire me to be a better person.

I have also become close with their parents. We are all part of a club that no one wants to belong to, but we are thankful to have each other. Kyla's parents are divorced, and her dad has had full custody of her since she was a toddler. I don't know much about her mother, but at the moment, they are not in contact. Kyla yearns for a mom to share her stories of life with, whether it's what boy she likes, the new outfit she just bought, her favorite reality

187

show—typical mom/daughter stuff. Since I have a teenage boy who is coming into puberty and wants nothing to do with his overly involved mom, I am more than happy to be a surrogate mom to Kyla. She touches a different place in my heart, as a daughter does differently from a son.

Hunter and Kyla spend several days a week together and she has gotten to know his friends. They all love her and have welcomed her into their tight-knit unit with open arms.

Kyla and I talk and text several times a day. She snuggles with me on the couch at night and fills me in on all of her secrets. We look at her Instagram and Facebook and talk about all the boys she once liked or dated.

On one of these precious nights, Kyla tells me she has a gift for me and hands me a small pendant in the shape of a dragonfly.

"I have carried this with me since I started treatment and I want you to have it," she says as she places it in my hand.

"Oh, honey, this is beautiful." I am looking at the small, metal dragonfly painted with a deep turquois color. "I love it, thank you."

I don't realize the significance of the gift at that moment, but would soon come to find out.

The next night when Kyla arrives, I can tell she has been crying. She cries a lot these days and I can tell her physical pain is worsening by the day.

"Sit down, kiddo. Let's talk," I instruct. "Tell me what is happening." I know something is terribly wrong and suspect it has something to do with her cancer. I also know that she will tell me when the time is right and I am praying that time is now.

I can't rush her, though. You see, kids with cancer feel a tremendous amount of guilt about their disease. They know that everyone they love is hurting and often feel responsible for that pain. They not only fear for themselves, but for their family and friends, too. Kyla would do anything to protect her loved ones and because of this, she kept the news she received days earlier to herself. The burden of it all became too much to bear and she finally surrenders.

"The cancer did not respond to the treatment, and I am out of options. I was told I have only a few months to live." She is bawling and saying, "I'm so sorry," over and over again.

All I can do is hold her. There are no words. There is no hope to remind her of. Her life is going to end, and I have to accept it, so I can help her accept it. I refuse to show her my deep sorrow and devastation, for I know she would hold herself responsible. I have also learned throughout Hunter's treatment that our children look to us for how to feel about certain things. When distressing news came, I knew I had to be calm about it and take the attitude of, "No problem…we got this!" Once Hunter knew I was okay, he was okay.

If I fall apart at this news, she would fall even deeper into despair and that is the last place I want her to go.

Now, it seems there are no more tears to shed, for the time being. We sit close together. I have known for some time that she is putting together a bucket list. I ask her if she would share it with me.

She smiles and reaches for the list from her backpack. The list reveals everything she ever wanted to do or experience, from a trip to Miami to dinners at fancy restaurants. I am happy she is willing to share it. Her friends and family come together and start planning trips, dinners, shopping, and many, many other things she wishes for. We know we need to work quickly, and we do. By the time she is too ill to travel, she has knocked off nearly half of the items on that list.

"I'm not ready," Kyla says to me one night. "There is still so much to do." She repeats this sentiment to many people close to her. She is truly anxious and I want to make it all go away.

"I know, honey, but don't forget, you have a lot of people who will be here to see this through." I respond, looking away so she doesn't see my tears streaming.

By this time, Kyla has started her own nonprofit organization called Movemountains.org. Her mission is to supply kids that are undergoing cancer treatment with a large canvas bag filled with all of the things that really helped her through chemo and radiation. The items include everything from her favorite super soft blanket to the lip balm that works best for chemo-chapped lips. It also contains items like body lotion, games, books she loves, and a host of other treats, all thoughtfully compiled with the age and gender of a child in mind.

Kyla works tirelessly on her project and wants nothing more than to see her vision and mission come to fruition. That was the kind of person she was. Even on her last days, she was thinking about others.

"Remember when I gave you that dragonfly?" she asks.

"You mean this one?" I pull it from my pocket and show it to her.

"Yes," she says with a little laugh. "That's the one. I have always loved what dragonflies represent, you know, transition from one thing to another. I was praying that I would transition from sick to healthy, but that didn't happen. So, when I found out that I would not survive this, I gave you the pendant. There is no use wishing upon it anymore, but I want you to think of me whenever you see a dragonfly, okay?"

I give her a tight hug and promise her that I will think of her every day, whether or not I see a dragonfly. "But if I do, I know it will be you, coming by to say hello." Kyla is so desperate for a drop of comfort that she smiles as I share this bittersweet promise.

Kyla and Hunter are spending a lot of time together. Three months pass and it is to be her last day of life in this world. Hunter spends over an hour alone with her, holding her hand. He never shares with me anything about that last visit with her, but I am certain she was at peace knowing he was with her.

When he walks out of her room, the hallway is filled with her family and a select few friends that she had requested to be there to see her off. There is not a dry eye as we watch Hunter walk toward us.

"Are you okay?" I ask.

"Yup."

He has been hardened by the losses in his life and has limited emotions left to share. He hugs Kyla's friends and relatives before we leave, knowing the next time we see them will be at her funeral.

By the time we arrive home, she has passed. Hunter is up in his room. I sit, sipping tea, and look out the dining room window. There is a dragonfly looking back at me.

One. Little. Pill.

"You don't have to see the whole staircase. Just take the first step."
—Martin Luther King

Epilogue

I marvel at what God has given to me. Last week I celebrated 19 years of sobriety. Next month, Hunter will reach the milestone of 10 years in remission. He is a grown, healthy, busy adult and I am blessed that we live close by and see each other often. My heart bursts with love and pride for him every day.

My parents also live close by and continue to be a beacon of love and support to both of us. I never take for granted how blessed I have been to have parents like mine.

The chaos and commotion of my life did not scare Kevin off, and we are still going strong. He has taught me how to live a full life and helped me to shed the fear I had been wearing like a wet fur coat for so many years. He freed me from the constant worry that plagued me, assuring me I will never face another battle of any kind, alone again. He is as constant as the northern star and continues to provide for me a safe refuge through every storm.

Although I would have never expected to experience so many trials when I decided to live a clean and sober life, I can clearly see how all the events unfolded exactly at the right time.

I believe that God had a hand in the timing for me to finally say enough is enough. God knew that Hunter would get cancer and suffer traumatizing loss, and that I would need to be clear-headed and strong during those years. God made sure I had many years in recovery before facing the challenges that were coming our way.

When I speak at a meeting or share my experience, strength, and hope with another addict, I often use a metaphor to help them understand the importance of the fellowship of AA and NA. Thinking of myself as a tree, every time I attend a meeting or practice the principles of the program, my roots grow deeper into the ground and my branches become fuller with hearty leaves. Every time a storm hits (which it will), the wind blows fiercely, trying to knock

A tight hug…two victors, different battles.

me over and take me down. The storm doesn't want me to be strong and healthy; its intention is to clear its path and, break me in half if it can. But my roots have grown deep and strong. I may bend and lose a few branches in the intensity of the storm, but I don't break.

Although watching Hunter battle cancer was immeasurably painful, I had many blessings bestowed on me that I otherwise may not have received. The most important and considerable was the solidification of my faith. I had always believed in God, but never *knew* Him. Today I not only know Him, but I *trust* him and His plan for me.

I know without a doubt that regardless of what life throws at me, I will be okay. I lean into Him every day and have learned to surrender my fears to Him. It's not always easy, but the alternative of holding onto fear and worry is far too heavy for me. Like they say: "I can't, God can, so I might as well let Him."

I continue to see dragonflies around me and there are days when I have seen *hundreds* of them swirling around me, their iridescent wings quietly fluttering, reminding me that our lost loved ones are never far from us. I watch them, knowing that this is a message from Kyla, letting me know she is free from pain and suffering and showing off her beautiful wings.

And then I'm reminded that I went through my own transformation. It's important for me to pause…to admire and appreciate my own beautiful, new wings. The ones I earned from living clean. Sobriety saved me from the nose-dive my life was taking, from a crash that would have destroyed my life, my son's life.

Take whatever you can take from my story that I've written here, because it's for you. By joining me as I walked my path from chaos and despair to peace and joy, I hope you learned some things you can take as lessons for what to avoid and what to embrace. Today is the perfect day to take a step towards more peace and joy in your life.

May God bless you and always hold you close.

*A brief moment in time
—Hunter before cancer,
with his dad in the good times*

*Me with Hunter, my sole reason to
give up the chase and enter rehab
a few months after this picture was taken*

*Hunter with Teeka
— Teeka saved me from relapse on that fateful night in 2013*

Kristen and me,
a fun little break from Step work

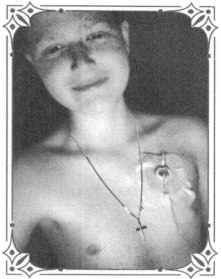

Hunter in hospital
– His white blood count was zero
for several days. The most scared
I had been for his life.

We Made It!
Hunter cleared his last chemo
and was discharged for the
last time on my birthday
—my favorite gift ever! (2013)

Ten years later...
A family celebration of
10 years in remission and
me being 10 years older
(and still clean and sober!)

Me with Hunter and my mom, holding hands after a 9-hour surgery in attempt to save his leg

Both Hunter and Robby in remission long enough to attend the Relay for Life event in Farmington, CT

Hunter with me, memorial golf tournament for Hunter's best friend Robby

Hunter and Kyla volunteering at the charity golf tournament in memory of Robby

Kyla, during one of her remissions.
I always think that this is
how she looks in Heaven.

the DRAGONFLY
CHARM

This very little dragonfly
will bring lightness
into your day,
it will help bring you joy,
as you travel along life's way.

This dragonfly reminds you
to be strong and
courageous too,
keep a positive attitude
in all that you do!

Kyla's dragonfly
—she carried this with her everywhere
until she gave it to me
to remember her by.

Me with Kristen, my first sponsor in my new life of recovery,
reunite to rekindle our special friendship after many years (2024)

Acknowledgments

This book would not be in existence if it weren't for Kevin, my dearest friend and partner, who gave me the gift of time to write and supported me in all the ways I needed. You continue to make all my dreams come true and I love being on this journey of life with you.

To my parents, George and Sande, who have always provided me safety and unconditional love, even when I didn't deserve it. You are the greatest example of love, loyalty, and family values I have ever known. You have given your family the beautiful gift of love, which will be passed on for generations to come.

Much gratitude to my lovely friend Kim Isabelle, whose excitement for this book was felt daily from 1500 miles away. Your faith is remarkable, and your light is as bright as sunshine. Thank you for always keeping me laughing!

BIG thanks to my editor and publisher, Barbara Dee, who helped me make my dream of writing this book come true. I am grateful to Linda Remley Gorman for taking the time to read my book and write a beautiful foreword. I am humbled by both of you.

For Robby, Kyla, and all the angels who fought valiantly for their lives— you are not forgotten. You will never be forgotten. You all inspire me every day to be a better person, to keep things in perspective, and never take life for granted. Your battle was not in vain.

To those who are fighting the disease of addiction (of any kind), I acknowledge you. I see you. I feel you. Please don't give up. You are loved, wanted, and needed.

Thank you to my Heavenly Father, my Savior Jesus Christ, my Angels and Spirit guides who gently steer me towards my life's purpose every day.

On the day I called, you answered me; My strength of soul you increased.
Psalm 138:3

About the Author

Deb Lawless-Miller's passion is helping people find renewed joy and purpose through life in recovery from substance use disorder. She remains an active participant in multiple support groups, frequently sharing her story of recovery and faith, including in service to women in prison or rehab centers.

She speaks on this topic to those in rehab, students, faith-based groups, mental health facilities, and all others needing information and inspiration.

In addition to her work in the community and her speaking engagements, she owns and operates Purpose Driven Life, LLC, helping small nonprofits to build a sustainable and effective organization.

Deb grew up in Avon, CT, and graduated from Quinnipiac University with a BA in Psychology. She now lives in Florida.

You are invited to visit: DebLawlessMiller.com